C000015750

KINGS & QUEENS

KINGS & QUEENS

Malcolm Day

RP

RYDON
PUBLISHING

A Rydon Publishing Book
35 The Quadrant
Hassocks
West Sussex
BN6 8BP

www.rydonpublishing.co.uk
www.rydonpublishing.com

Revised edition first published by Rydon Publishing in 2018
First published by David & Charles in 2011

Copyright © Rydon Publishing 2018

Malcolm Day has asserted his right to be identified as the author of this
work in accordance with the Copyright, Designs and Patents Act, 1998.

All rights reserved. No part of this publication may be reproduced, stored
in a retrieval system, or transmitted in any form or by any means, electronic
or mechanical, by photocopying, recording or otherwise, without prior
permission in writing from the publisher.

This book is sold subject to the condition that it shall not, by trade or
otherwise, be lent, re-sold, hired out, or otherwise circulated without the
publisher's prior consent in any form of binding or cover other than that
in which it is published and without a similar condition including this
condition being imposed on the subsequent purchaser.

The designs in this book are copyright and should not be made for resale.

A CIP catalogue record for this book is available from the British Library.

ISBN: 978-1-910821-21-3

Printed in Poland by BZGraf SA

CONTENTS

INTRODUCTION

When Prince Charles, though not actually king, but acting in the full role of heir apparent, objected to the proposed building of a modernist extension to the National Gallery, his remark that it would be like 'a monstrous carbuncle on the face of a much loved friend' in many respects could only have been uttered by one blessed with royal prerogative. Anyone dispensable would never have dared to object with such forceful condemnation. Whatever our feelings about the right he might have had to make such a comment, the fact that he made it underlies the age-old reality that royalty knows no limits.

Until they were reined in by Parliament, British monarchs historically have done whatever pleases them, sometimes regretfully and to their undoing. But it is just this unbounded wilfulness that provides us with an enduring fascination for the royals. Sovereigns were for so long a rule unto themselves – and we surely envy such unrestrained liberty! Certainly to read about the eccentric, the bombastic, the outrageous deeds in these lives adds a vivid streak of colour to the mundane sphere of humanity, like blue veins through a cheese.

Indeed it is royalty's idea of self-importance – of being accountable to noone – that has set them apart. No wonder the notion of blue blood makes us smile: it is absurd yet appealing, and in a way it perfectly symbolises the historically held belief that our kings and queens came gift-wrapped in divine protection. Absolute power was bestowed in equal measure on the weak as on the mighty, the vain as the earnest, the desultory as the ambitious. Whatever earthly sin they may commit, deadly or venal, it was as nothing so long as blue blood coursed through the veins of its perpetrator.

Bizarre though the idea of such infallibility might seem today, the concept was widespread in the ancient world. England was a Christian kingdom founded on the early Israelite tradition of anointed kingship. It should be no surprise that a monarch such as Charles I would do away with any obstacle to his rule, including a testy government he thought more nuisance than useful.

The king's divine right to rule was taken very seriously. Only a body with such certainty of religious conviction as the Puritans possessed could be confident of challenging such authority. However our kings and queens have viewed their role, their attitudes to the monarchy have varied enormously – some, such as Henry VI and George VI, have even wished they had no such blessing.

It is the curious and the unusual in these royal lives that come into focus in this book, from the eccentric domestic routines of George II to young Eadwig caught by St Dunstan in a *ménage a trois*; or Queen Anne's bearing of 17 children none of whom would survive to inherit her crown. The scope of the book is not to produce a series of potted biographies, dwelling on the well read. Some extraordinary facts might be familiar to us but are worth the re-telling because they are just that. Sometimes figures such as William and Mary we might feel are familiar to us, yet other, lesser-known facts about them can be learnt that cast these players in quite a different light.

In the case of this double act, for instance, is it known that Mary dreaded marrying her Dutch cousin and wept with sorrow on their wedding day? Questions and unsolved mysteries still abound, despite the best investigations of historians who will disagree, and simply admit to not knowing what precisely motivated some actions. The jury is still out on Richard III, for example. What was going through his mind when he decided, fatefully, to take those two princes captive and execute them. And why was Elizabeth I so envious of her imprisoned sister Mary Queen of Scots?

Every king and queen of England is included, except for the young Prince in the Tower, whose interest is related in the entry on Richard III. Some Scottish monarchs have been selected, and I apologise that space has not allowed more. There is also an admixture of mythical kings and queens – the likes of Trojan Brutus and King Lear – who I feel hold a place in our culture, representing as they do the earliest traditions of sovereignty in Britain.

Malcolm Day

Refugee from Ancient Israel?

How the Trojan Brutus may have been Britain's first Jew

The man credited with founding the ancient nation of Britons is by tradition descended from the Trojans. According to popular legend, the great grandson of Aeneas (refugee from Troy and founder of Italy) wandered westwards through western Europe and sailed up the River Dart to Totnes. From here Brutus led his band of cohorts to conquer the island by defeating the native Albion giants led by Gogmagog.

If we look at the ancestral lineage of Brutus, there are interesting parallels to be made. As grandson of Aeneas he would have been descended from Dardanus,

the founder of Troy. Now some traditions claim that Dardanus is a linguistic alternative to Dara or Darda, mentioned in the Bible in I Chronicles 2:6 as the grandson of Judah, founder of one of the twelve tribes of Israel. Therefore Brutus may have a biblical pedigree and kinship with the Chosen People.

It is thought that the Ten Lost Tribes of the northern kingdom of Israel may have followed in the wake of Brutus and made their way to Britain where they settled. A scriptural clue to this migration is given in the apocryphal II Esdras (chapter 13: 40–47), which says they 'go forth into a further country … there was a great way to go, namely, of a year and a half: and the same region is called Arzareth.' British-Israelites say that Arzareth, though literally meaning 'another land', actually refers to a land in southern Russia north of the Black Sea, to be identified with Cimmeria. In turn, this name developed into 'Cymry', the name for the Welsh people. So Brutus and his tribesmen were the forebears of the Celts of Wales and southern England.

Indeed, British-Israelites claim that

all the ancestral natives of Britain are of Israelite origin. The idea, based on the prophecy of Ezekiel, that all the dispersed elements of Israel would one day be reunited in a single nation in the Promised Land took hold in Britain on the grounds of this belief. And to some extent a lobby for its cause forced the momentum towards the formation of the British Mandate for Palestine in 1920.

Bladud
Legendary Celtic founder of Bath with Athenian arts

When Bath became the most fashionable city in Georgian England, the sensation at the heart of its appeal was its miraculous spring water. A vast amount of water gushed out every day and was somehow heated to a temperature of 49°C (120°F). Not only was it a pleasant and sociable recreation to wade about in such an element, these waters had a reputation from ancient times of possessing a curative quality.

Legend has it that a ninth-century BC Celtic pretender to the throne, Bladud, was responsible for discovering these special springs when caring for a herd of pigs. He noticed those that wallowed in the mud there seemed to develop healthier skin. Famously, on having a go himself Bladud discovered that he too lost the leprosy that had bedevilled his skin and hitherto disqualified him from inheriting the throne as descendant of King Brutus. This much is known.

Certain conjecture, however, has it that the fantastic heat and minerality generated from the earth was in fact the product of Bladud's own scientific experimentation. It is documented that as a bright youth he was sent to Athens to learn at the feet of Greek philosophers. He is said

to have acquired advanced scientific knowledge there and returned to Britain with four scholars and founded a university at Stamford in Lincolnshire.

With his new skill Bladud is believed to have created two huge 'tuns' (barrels with a capacity of 252 gallons), filled with burning brass, and two more containing salt, brimstone and fire. These four tuns he buried in the ground and they provided the source of the magical effluent of Bath.

Not surprisingly, the waters were regarded as poisonous and certainly not to be drunk. Only a craze such as was likely to happen in the heyday of Georgian society could induce the gullible to 'take the waters', as they did in their droves, and then take to their beds!

Liberated from the curse of leprosy, Bladud was able to claim his rightful crown as king. He is said to have ruled for 20 years before dying in a flying accident, hence his depiction sometimes with wings. Bladud was succeeded by King Lear.

Tragic Loss Regained
The alternative account to Shakespeare on King Lear

The premature death of King Bladud from a flying accident left the throne to his young son, Leir. Made famous by William Shakespeare as King Lear, he ruled for near on 60 years according to Geoffrey of Monmouth, who places the British king in parallel time to the prophet Elijah of Ancient Israel.

The story told by Shakespeare is well known but it differs from the legendary account in its ending. As in the play, Leir has no son for an heir. The problem of dividing his kingdom equally among his three daughters and his test of their love, which unjustly excludes his favourite youngest daughter, Cordelia, is common to both accounts.

But the realisation of his misjudgement and reconciliation with Cordelia, who nurses her half-crazed father back to health, leads Leir to form a successful alliance with the king of Gaul, Aganippus. Together, they invade Britain and, unlike Shakespeare's version, overthrow the dukes of Albany and Cornwall who have married his two other daughters respectively. Leir reclaims the British throne and rules for three more years until his natural death. He is succeeded to the throne by Cordelia. So Monmouth's version has no tragic ending with a distraught Lear holding the dead body of Cordelia who has committed suicide.

Who Made Britain's First Laws?
Our bard says it was King Mulmutius

Centuries before the Romans arrived and imposed their judicial system on Britain, the land seldom had any real sense of political unity. Kingdoms came and went, most claiming descendency from the first British king, Brutus. And when King Lear's squabbling offspring contrived their own demise, early Celtic society was once again plunged into chaos. The poor and the weak fell to the mercy of their overlords as tribal chieftains warred constantly for supremacy. Now Tudor historians claim there was one monarch among

this unruly ancient rabble who broke the mould.

On vanquishing his enemies in the fifth century BC, a great Celtic warrior king, by the name of Dunvallo Molmutius, determined not only to reunite the broken nation but to give his subjects a measure of protection against ruthless power moguls. To signify this new kind of sovereignty the king had a new golden crown made and instituted a canon of rights which in some ways anticipates Magna Carta of medieval times.

This extraordinarily enlightened monarch so impressed William Shakespeare that he figured on the lips of King Cymbeline in his play of the same name:

Mulmutius made our laws,
Who was the first of Britain which did put
His brows within a golden crown, and call'd
Himself a king.
(Cymbeline, Scene 1)

In his long reign lasting 45 years, Molmutius laid down various principles by which society would be bound together in mutual respect and security. All peasants, for example, had the right to work. Even if they were in debt, their creditors could not come and seize their plough or other working implement and so deprive them of their livelihood.

Laws were established to prevent crime. And temples were to be sanctuaries, inviolable spaces where any individual was entitled to safe refuge.

It is said that the Molmutine Laws were written in a British language, later translated into Latin, and then adapted by King Alfred to form part of his constitution.

Lud, Lover of London
An early town planner

Though it is our Trojan ancestor Brutus who is credited with founding London, the man who had a passion for the city was King Lud, the last monarch of any significance in the old realm of Britain.

Lud was a pioneering town planner. With great gusto this visionary Celt set his heart on building a city to rival any other in the known world. Recalling his ancestry, he endeavoured to turn what was an unremarkable town into a fabulous citadel worthy of its romantic name, New Troy. Ramparts were thrown up, towers added at strategic points. Within the walls, building regulations were imposed to ensure only the highest of standards in architecture – no monstrous carbuncles allowed. Nightly his love

of the city overflowed in grand banquets and celebrations. Indeed, so closely associated with the city did King Lud become that it was renamed after him as Caer Lud, later corrupted to Caer Lundein. In time the 'Caer' was dropped and the result 'London', which the Romans turned into Londinium.

After his death Lud was buried near a gateway to the city named after him, Ludgate. A statue that used to stand on the gate now graces the porch of the church of St Dunstan-in-the-West in Fleet Street in commemoration of his proud endeavour.

Celtic Charioteers Shock Caesar
How Cassivellaunus stalled the mighty Romans

It took two invasions by Julius Caesar to subdue the Britons. The first effort, in 55 CE, may have been little more than a reconnaissance trip. At any rate, Caesar's galleons floundered on the Kent coast in the unfamiliar Atlantic high tides and he made little headway into the interior. Deciding to cut his losses before the

winter set in, the Roman leader beat a hasty retreat back to Gaul. The following year Caesar tried again, this time with a massive task force of five legions, amounting to some 30,000 crack soldiers and 2000 cavalry, all aboard a fleet of 800 ships.

What Caesar learned on his first trip was that the Britons, though fierce were a squabbling lot and may well prove to be their own worst enemy. He hoped the mere sight of such a powerful army would induce their surrender. However, what he encountered in this second invasion was a determined resistance on a united front. The tribes of southeast Britain had put aside their differences and thrown in their lot with King Cassivellaunus of the

Catuvellauni tribe.

Whilst they had nowhere near the numbers fielded by the enemy, the Celts had become a skilled fighting unit with one weapon unfamiliar to the Romans: the chariot. Cassivellaunus was able to muster 4000 chariots as well as foot soldiers. In his report of the invasion, Caesar described how the Celts used their chariots in battle. The driver would control the two horses and the warrior behind him would hurl javelins at the enemy before leaping off to fight on foot. Ever ready to give honour where it is due, Caesar commended the slickness of the operation:

… they display in battle the speed of horse, the firmness of infantry; and by daily practice and exercise attain to such expertness that they are accustomed, even on a declining and steep place, to check their horses at full speed, and manage and turn them in an instant.

As well as their accomplished charioteering the Celts employed clever guerrilla tactics to disturb the Roman advance. Cassivellaunus planted sharp stakes - the ancient equivalent of mines – in the bed of the Thames and along the river banks. When enemy ships sailed up the estuary, many were holed and sunk. However, the overwhelming strength of the Roman force proved too great and once they had made headway across the land north of the Thames ruled by Cassivellaunus, his temporary allies began to desert him and side with the Romans. The embattled king had no choice but to negotiate a surrender.

Tribute and hostages were agreed, but Caesar departed without leaving behind a single legionary to enforce the treaty. Did he ever receive the tribute? In the end, the question might be asked whether Caesar's expedition was really more about pride and completing unfinished business than about greed.

Perhaps the reason why the Romans did not return to these shores for nearly another century was that those Britons were a tricky lot to handle.

You've Never Had It So Good

Rare peace and prosperity under Cymbeline

The king named Cymbeline by William Shakespeare had a more down-to-earth name in the real world of the Celts: Cunobelinus, or 'Hound of Belinus'. Belinus was a Celtic god who Geoffrey of Monmouth claims helped in the sack of Rome in 390 BC. Cymbeline was Belinus's descendent in kind. By defeating his neighbours Cymbeline made himself king over most of southern Britain, according to the Latin historian Suetonius.

For 30 years Cymbeline brought peace and prosperity to his kingdom. He adopted the Roman centre Camulodunum (Colchester) as his capital, for his homeland was the Essex of today. Being close to the Channel, he encouraged commerce with the continent and a flourishing trade developed. Wheat, cattle, hunting dogs, hides, slaves and metals were exported in return for such luxuries as wine, fine robes, jewellery and ornamental glass for his barons. In all necessities Cymbeline's subjects were self-sufficient.

When the Romans tried to exact arrears of tribute from the British realm, they were given short shrift. As the king's stepson pronounced in Shakespeare's play, Cymbeline:

> *Britain is*
> *A world by itself, and we will*
> *Nothing pay*
> *For wearing our own noses.*

A Charmed Life
Despite heavy defeats Caractacus has the last word in Rome

Determined and fearless though King Caractacus of the Catuvellauni tribe was reputed to be, he was never likely to prevail against the awesome power of the Romans. As the Latin legions massed their ranks on the northern shores of Gaul in 43 CE, ready to invade Britain, Caractacus called his fierce warriors to arms.

Despite brave resistance, Caractacus and his outnumbered compatriots suffered a heavy defeat. The king and some of his men managed to

escape westwards. They laid low for five years before rising again, this time allied with the Celtic tribes of mid-Wales, the Ordovices and Silures. Together they conducted a guerrilla warfare that stalled the Roman advance until 51 CE.

A final battle saw Caractacus's comrades put to the sword and his wife, children and brothers captured. Yet again Caractacus escaped, and thought he had found a safe haven with the Brigantes of the Pennines. But their queen, Cartimandua, secretly formed an alliance with the Romans and betrayed him into their hands.

Taken prisoner to face trial in Rome, Caractacus could only fear the worst. But such valour and bearing as the British king displayed was unusual to behold in an enemy of the imperial court. Legend has it that when Claudius confronted him, Caractacus asked the Roman emperor, 'Why do you wish to conquer my impoverished country when you already rule Rome?' Claudius was so impressed at his courage that he pardoned the British king and gave him the freedom of Rome where he spent the rest of his days with his family.

It is said that his father, Cunobelinus (Shakespeare's Cymbeline), met the apostle Paul while in Rome and was converted to Christianity. He then took the faith back to his homeland and became the first Christian to step foot in Britain.

Holy War
The sacred hare of Boudicca

The account of Boudicca's revolt, the largest ever in Britain against the Romans, is a patriotic landmark in British history. Rich in symbolism – ferocious female leader crushing mighty male-dominated Rome – has resonated through the centuries whenever our small island has faced a powerful enemy from the continent. The statue on London's Embankment of Boudicca 'loftily charioted', in Tennyson's phrase, is a constant reminder of the achievement. Her rising up in fury at Rome's confiscation of her deceased husband's lands, the rightful inheritance of her

two daughters, not to mention the alleged atrocities committed to all three females, fired a rebellion of such extraordinary intensity as to reach mythical proportions.

If the rebellion was principally an act of vengeance against a hated overlord, how did Boudicca galvanise her forces so effectively? Were they so incensed anyway that she merely had to say the word and off they would charge like bats from hell? No, for the like of this had not been seen before. Clues to the answer lie in the assembled army on the eve of battle. The Roman historian Dio Cassius gives us the only extant account of the occasion.

Accordingly, Boudicca addressed her East Anglian tribe, the Iceni, at great length, preparing them for their onslaught the next day on Camulodunum (Colchester), the Roman capital in Britain. Dio paints an awesome picture of the Celtic queen: 'in appearance, terrifying, in the glance of her eye most fierce, and her voice was harsh; a great mass of the tawniest hair fell to her hips.' In her speech she reminds the assembled people vividly of their recent treatment at the hand of the Romans: she talks of the gulf between freedom and slavery, how the Britons have suffered since the Romans occupied their land. It is not too late to rise up, if only for the sake of their children, lest they too are raised in bondage.

Then, at the end of her speech, Boudicca suddenly produces from beneath the folds of her bright tunic a hare, which she releases. As it darts away, the hare is observed to run 'in an auspicious direction', to the loud cheering of the crowd. Clearly this represented a favourable omen for the uprising.

Spirit of the hare

The hare was sacred to the ancient Celts, who saw it as a powerful spirit associated with their goddess Andraste. In ancient mythology the hare was generally believed to have a strong connection with the moon goddess (possibly because at full moon the shape of the animal can be discerned within it). The animal was endowed with lunar characteristics, such as fertility, rebirth, transformation, as well as hidden knowledge. It acted as an intermediary between heaven and earth, and its movements on the ground were used for divining change in the future.

Having received this godly revelation, Boudicca then prayed: 'I thank thee, Andraste, and call upon thee as woman speaking to woman.' It is thought that Andraste was the war-goddess of the Iceni, and in so addressing herself to the deity, Boudicca was assuming a joint role as priestess, prophetess and war leader. She was effectively embarking on a Holy War against the Romans – a war which, it had been prophesied, the Iceni would win.

No wonder her people were so committed to the cause. With the divine stamp of approval, they surely could not fail. Thus fired with fanatic fervour, Boudicca's army rampaged southwards at daybreak and overwhelmed the bemused Romans, first in Camulodunum, then Londinium (London), and finally Verulamium (St Albans). It is said that Boudicca charged with the holy hare tucked into her cloak. Alas, once the Romans had recovered from the shock they mustered their considerable forces and retaliated in kind. The Iceni suffered a heavy defeat and Boudicca resorted to taking poison rather than face the humiliation of an inevitably gruesome punishment.

Did Constantine the Great Have a British Grandfather?
Could it have been Old King Cole?

Legends abound about King Cole, a merry old soul who lived the life of Reilly in Colchester. Wine, pipes and fiddlers' tunes are the stuff of a nursery rhyme that gave colour to this character, supposedly once the king of Britain. Ancient lore is often far-fetched but it can also spring from a grain of truth. Is there any to be had here?

According to tradition, Coel (or Cole), Duke of Colchester, attacked and defeated King Asclepiodotus and took the British crown for himself. As Britain was a protectorate at the time, Rome sent over senator Constantius to negotiate, and a settlement was agreed. Coel's rich living got the better of him, however, and he died

within a month of the treaty being formed. Feeling the need to grab the tiller in the sudden absence of a captain, Constantius assumed control, though not the throne. To become popular with his new subjects he is said to have married Coel's lovely daughter, Helena (known to posterity as St Helen).

Now we do know that Constantius ruled Britain, in fact for 11 years, and that he married a woman named Helena. She bore him a son, Constantine, future great emperor of Rome (and reputedly in later life discovered the True Cross in Jerusalem). Some traditions maintain Helena was British, some even say she was a British princess. If that was so, was King Cole her father?

There was clearly a need to establish Helena's status in British royalty. It is Henry of Huntingdon we have to thank for first making the connection in English records, in 1129, between Helena, 'mother of Constantine', and 'King Coel, ruler of Colchester'. A noble figure by the name of Coel probably did exist, as a ruler in northern Britain, but his connection with Colchester and, even more tenuous, with Helena, has to be consigned to fiction.

It transpires that the real Helena was a barmaid from Drepanum in Bithynia (now part of Turkey). Constantius met her on a drinking spree, married her and indeed divorced her before even setting foot in Britain to take charge. His son Constantine joined him there and when Constantius died was sworn emperor at York.

Great Mounted Archer
Arthur's role in a Somerset zodiac

For all the associations of Arthur with Glastonbury, this connection did not exist until monks at Glastonbury Abbey claimed in the twelfth century to have discovered the tomb of King Arthur. Prior to then, even the great legend-maker Geoffrey of Monmouth did not identify Glastonbury with Avalon, the mythical Isle of Apples, where Arthur traditionally was laid to rest.

It was the medieval French writer Malory who really set the romantic flame alight in Le Morte d'Arthur by developing the legends of Arthur and

the Knights of the Round Table.

Yet for all the dismissiveness of modern scholars that Arthur was at best no more than a Celtic warrior fending off invading Saxons, Glastonbury Tor does appear majestic above the Somerset Levels as though designed to be a grand cenotaph to a national hero. The Tor has a mythic quality about it and has prompted a good deal of research into its significance in the landscape surrounding it.

A theory was put forward by Katherine Maltwood in the 1920s that the Arthurian story was in fact

The geographic zodiac, according to Maltwood

a literary reflection of an astrological mystery embedded in the landscape. She identified topographical features that seemed to be aligned in a circle. This arrangement, she claims, is the reality behind the Round Table, which can be seen as a kind of terrestrial zodiac – a gigantic map of the stars on the ground. Features such as water courses, ancient roads, dykes and woodlands are configured in such a way as to indicate astrological characters. Arthur, for instance, is imaged as a mounted archer, the tenth sign of the zodiac.

Sceptics make counter-claims that these geographical features did not all exist at the same time and so cannot be said to form a coherent whole. And no conventional archaeologists support the theory.

Others, however, have raised further celestial speculations, including the idea that seven hills around Glastonbury make a configuration resembling the constellation known as the Great Bear, or the Plough. In line with this, it is pointed out that Arthur's name stems from the Welsh Arth Fawr, meaning Great Bear.

The Mystery of Sutton Hoo
Was this the state funeral of the Anglo-Saxon king Redwald?

In 1939 an archaeological dig unearthed a burial of extraordinary magnificence. Beneath the windswept mound that stood like the English version of an ancient Egyptian pyramid near the coast of Suffolk, an excavation revealed the outline of a huge boat – 27 metres (90 feet) in length, 4 metres (14 feet) across – together with a host of precious artefacts. This amazingly rich find suddenly threw open a window on a world of Anglo-Saxon civilisation previously unknown.

The original timber structure had all but disintegrated, but what remained to indicate the shape of the boat were perfectly preserved rows of rivets. In the centre was a chamber with a helmet, sword of gold and garnet fittings, spears, battle-axes, a shield with bird and dragon figures, bowls, silver spoons, a lyre, chess set, several pieces of beautifully crafted jewellery and forty Merovingian coins from the continent. The

First royal sceptre

collection taken together pointed to one conclusion: an elaborate funeral had been performed in the form of a ship-burial. Just as Egyptian pharaohs were launched into the next world when interred in a pyramid, an important figure had received similar treatment in an Anglo-Saxon context. But who? A king, a druid?

One problem immediately emerged after the discovery: there was no body. No skeleton even. It was said that Henry VIII's men had dug here for treasure and indeed Elizabethan diggers' snacks and a tool had been found. Nearby, towards the end of the 17th century, a gold crown was unearthed too, but was sold and melted down.

The location of the burial was a known centre of East Anglian royal power. The Merovingian coins found in a purse have been dated c.625 CE, the period given by the Anglo-Saxon historian Bede for the death of King Redwald. Anglo-Saxon society was a loose confederation of kingdoms and on that premise alone many kings could be candidates. But one king alone had the title 'Bretwalda', or Overlord, and at the time of Sutton Hoo it was Redwald.

THE BRETWALDA

This somewhat enigmatic title is associated with Anglo-Saxon kingship. Originally it meant 'over-king', the king who rules other kings, and was probably nothing more than honorary. But in time its status acquired power and the title came to mean 'Britain-ruler'. Because early Anglo-Saxon society roughly consisted of a heptarchy of seven kingdoms – Kent, Sussex (South Saxons), Wessex (West Saxons), Essex (East Saxons), East Anglians, Mercia (Midlands), and Northumbria (northern Anglians) – there arose the need for an overall ruler. The term originated in Old High German and was imported when the Saxon tribes migrated to Britain. Unlike modern dynastic succession the title was not hereditary, but seemed to be granted by common consent. Quite what were the grounds for that entitlement is unclear. It is possible that the term carried some form of investiture of the god Woden, from which Anglo Saxon kings derived their divine right to rule. Whatever was the full significance of the Bretwalda, the title marked a key stage in the development of the English institution of monarchy.

The grave-goods were undoubtedly of supreme quality, and the regalia found may well have belonged to the Bretwalda. But one item in particular shone out as pointing to a figure of Redwald's status. This was the whetstone, a finely crafted sceptre made of the hardest stone. It is decorated with mysterious male faces and topped by a black disc surmounted by a stag with fine arcing antlers. Stags were symbols of royalty. Whetstones were found in Swedish graves of this period, but none as large as this one, two feet long. One eminent archaeologist described it as 'monstrous, a unique savage thing; and

inexplicable except as a symbol proper to the king himself.'

So if it was indeed King Redwald's funeral, why no trace of a body? Some say the ship was only a cenotaph (monument of the dead), and that a pyre nearby would have cremated the body. Even forensic experts could find no human remains. However, what was discovered was a complete set of iron coffin fittings. These formed a perfect rectangular outline of a wooden coffin around which the grave goods were neatly arranged. A scientific explanation for the missing body maintains that acid sand in which the boat lay could have gradually rotted away the bones, even the teeth.

Romantic speculation about Sutton Hoo is further fuelled by the poem *Beowulf*, written much later but which perhaps preserves some of the memories of such a momentous event. A great pyre was built and after the body and weapons were consumed in flames,

> ... *the Great people began to construct a mound on a headland ...*
> *It was their hero's memorial; what remained from the fire*

They housed inside it …
And they buried torques in the
barrow, and jewels
And a trove …

Little is known about the life of Redwald. Bede says he converted to Christianity in Kent but on his return to East Anglia reverted to his old pagan worship. Perhaps his burial combined elements of both faiths.

First Christian English King
Ethelbert sees the Roman Church as key to political power

After the collapse of Rome as a political power, Britain became a two-sided society: on the one hand there were the Romano-British people who clung to the institutions and culture that had evolved over the last 500 years, and on the other hand there were the Anglo-Saxon settlers who exerted control over the land. With the latter came their pagan beliefs and customs.

The Anglo-Saxon world of the sixth century was one of dragons and witches, and its kings all claimed descent from the Germanic god Woden with all his magical power.

At about the same time, across the Channel, Gaul had been taken over by a barbarian people, the Franks, who spoke a similar language to the Saxons, coming as they did from Germany. But the culture which prevailed in the land which took their name, France, was a good deal more refined than its Anglo-Saxon counterpart, and more powerful too,

having quickly expanded into an empire. Much of the Gallic tradition continued to be observed by the people, including its Christian faith.

Eyeing the opportunity

Now Anglo-Saxon kings did not have much status in Europe, and Ethelbert, though bretwalda (see page 26), was envious of the Franks' success. He wished not only to establish a strong reign in his own land but also to extend his influence abroad. With this in mind, he married the Frankish princess Bertha. But part of the condition of that union, imposed by her family, was that Ethelbert become a Christian like his wife. And here Ethelbert saw a political opportunity.

It was put to Pope Gregory the Great that the English were willing to be baptised, and to this end he dispatched a mission led by Augustine in 597. Now Ethelbert was a cautious man, as well as shrewd. On their arrival he held the missionaries on the Island of Thanet in Kent while he assessed this new faith. Not wanting to risk being overpowered by its god and priests, he made them present themselves in the open air, so that

any magic spell they might try to cast would disperse the more easily.

Ethelbert was impressed by the ceremony, with its elaborate dress, symbols and music. Knowing how much the Franks had benefited from having Roman Christian subjects, he duly allowed the papal envoys to go about their business. It is said, they baptised 10,000 new converts in Kent over Christmas. And Ethelbert could see the willingness with which his English subjects embraced their new religion.

Much about the Roman Church appealed to Ethelbert, steeped as he was in crude Anglo-Saxon paganism: its law, its Latin liturgy, its massive churches built of stone, and perhaps most of all the absolute supremacy of its leader.

If only Ethelbert himself would convert, Augustine beseeched, all this would be available to him, as king of Christian England. A wry smile must have graced Ethelbert's face as he finally took the oath of allegiance.

First ever document in English

Indeed so enthusiastic did Ethelbert's support of the Church become that he commissioned the first cathedral of St Paul's to be built (alas destroyed by fire in the tenth century).

He is also thought to have written the first ever document in English, in the oldest form of the language we have. Almost immediately after converting, Ethelbert insisted on issuing a code of laws in a language his people could understand. Augustine (who would become the first Archbishop of Canterbury) no doubt helped him draft the form of it, but its content is undoubtedly Anglo-Saxon.

Dyke Twice the Length of Hadrian's Wall
But why did the great Offa build one at all?

King Offa of Mercia must go down in English history as one of the most feared monarchs of the Dark Ages:

… in Mercia there ruled a mighty king called Offa, who struck all the kings and regions around him with terror. He it was who ordered the great dyke to be constructed between Wales and Mercia, stretching from sea to sea. (Bishop Asser, On the Deeds of King Alfred)

Offa is best known today for his dyke that stretches from the Irish Sea to the Bristol Channel. Yet in his day no record was made of it. In fact the extract above, written by Bishop Asser, was the first written record, put down some 100 years later. Even by today's standards the enterprise – part ditch, part rampart – is hugely impressive. It still stands six metres (20 feet) high in places and forms most of the border between Wales and England. But historians disagree about why it was built. Did it mark an agreed frontier? Or was it a fortification to be used as a Mercian command base from which to attack the Welsh?

The organization and labour involved must have been colossal. In a concerted programme, thousands of Anglo-Saxon peasants, perhaps drawn from different regions, would have assembled on the border country. They brought with them their horses and carts, tents, spades, axes, hammers, weapons, and set to work digging a ditch eight metres (25 feet) deep and 20 metres (65 feet) wide. Oxen hauled heavy ploughs to help turn up the earth. Everything they excavated was heaped up to form a huge rampart.

Throughout the spring, summer and probably the autumn, in about 787 CE, gangs of workmen would have been assigned piecemeal right along the 135 miles of dyke, camping out at night and labouring by day, like the railway navvies of the 19th century. Where the topography made alignment difficult, large beacons were set up on hilltops to ensure a continuous line. With a visibility range of up to 20 miles, these miniature lighthouses acted as a warning system against Welsh raids; indeed the system continued in use up to Elizabethan times when

it served to alert the nation of the approaching Spanish Armada.

Running along the top of the dyke was a wooden palisade, with stone bastions, the entire length broken only by occasional gateways for traders to pass through. Marshalls on horseback would have monitored progress, and sometimes among them figured the fearsome King Offa. Only someone with the regal clout he clearly possessed could have ensured such a project was completed. And completed it was within the year.

Megalomania

Although the whole enterprise is shrouded somewhat in mystery, we know something of the man who envisioned this extraordinary feat. Offa was a single-minded and determined leader. He was quite capable of seeing off any rival or obstruction that might bar his way, casually applying as much brutality as necessary.

For example, he had designs on Kent because of its trading gateway to the continent. The Church had considerable power in this region through its possession of the see of Canterbury. But Offa did not let this

stand in his way and devised a suitable stunt. Two papal legates were invited to a Council of the English Church. After some intense debate Offa won the day and had Lichfield, located in the heartland of Mercia, raised to an archbishopric whose incumbent would bound to support his elector.

Another indication of the king's megalomania was the coinage minted in his day. Offa had the silver penny enlarged and upgraded. His image appears to be modelled on the form of King David of ancient Israel. Following the tradition established there of ordained kingship, Offa had his son anointed as a divinely approved heir. Vast quantities of his coinage were struck and used to trade with the expanding economy of France – monetary inflation had never been so rampant.

Perhaps Offa's ploy was essentially one of safeguarding his border with the turbulent Welsh so that he could concentrate his energies on spreading his influence across the Channel.

First Saxon King of England
An unpromising start sees Egbert rise to the top

One of many victims of the mighty Offa, King of Mercia, was a young heir to the throne of Wessex. Fearing for his life, Egbert fled to France to seek refuge at the court of Emperor Charlemagne. Egbert bided his time there until a propitious moment at the beginning of the ninth century when he could return from exile and claim the throne of Wessex with relative ease.

A series of effective rebellions had undermined the overarching power of Mercia that had existed since the days of Offa. In the emerging free for all Wessex stepped up to become the supreme kingdom. Egbert, who was widely regarded as grand liberator, was then hailed in 825 as overall ruler – the very first king of a united Anglo-Saxon England.

Thus brought to a conclusion the several lines of kings that had comprised the seven separate Anglo-Saxon kingdoms. Kent had 18 kings up to Egbert; East Anglia had 16 kings, ending with St Edmund, after whom Bury St Edmunds in Hertfordshire is named; Essex had 15 kings; Sussex nine kings; Mercia 15 kings; Northumbria 25 kings; and Wessex 19 kings.

The Mystique of Scone
Kenneth MacAlpine inaugurates Scottish monarchy

At a time when the legendary Brutus ruled his kingdom in southern Britain, a northern people known as the Picts held an independent realm, now Scotland. The Scots were confined to a small region known as Dalriada in Argyll, sometimes controlled by the Picts. Over many centuries the Scots grew more numerous and powerful until, one day in the ninth century, when the Pictish accession was in doubt, the king of the Scots, Kenneth McAlpine, made a bid for the throne on the ground that he was slightly Pictish himself. He devised a devilish plot to succeed.

McAlpine met the Pictish leaders at their sacred centre of Scone, near Perth, to discuss the succession.

Inviting them to a banquet afterwards, he seated the nobles on benches placed above trap doors. When all were comfortable, he gave the order for supporting bolts to be drawn away sending the hapless Picts to a cellar below where waiting guards slaughtered them.

Having eliminated all his rivals to the throne in one fell swoop, McAlpine was free to rule a new kingdom of the Scots, traditionally called Albany, for it constituted the part of Albion north of the border drawn from the Clyde to the Forth which the Romans never conquered. From then on, this northern land was united under the Scots and also came to incorporate Strathclyde, a kingdom ruled at the time by the Welsh.

Stone of destiny
It was McAlpine who instituted the so-called Stone of Destiny in order to invest his rule with legitimacy, even divine authority. A sacred stone said to be the one on which the biblical Jacob once rested his head and dreamed of the descendants of Israel, had been brought to Ireland, according to legend, by an eastern

princess, named Tea. She married an Irish king and the stone featured in coronation rituals as the Stone of Destiny. This holy but bulky unhewn rock was brought over to Iona by Prince Fergus, founder of Dalriada. McAlpine now carried it on to Scone.

The stone was set up in a throne on which McAlpine and every successive monarch of Scotland would sit to receive the crown. The stone of Scone became an integral part of the mystique of Scottish royal legitimacy. In 1296, the victorious English king Edward I removed the stone to Westminster after conquering Scotland. The Scots say that wherever the stone is a Scot shall rule. This belief was vindicated in 1603 when James VI of Scotland was also crowned James I of England.

The King Who Forgave his Enemies
Alfred the Great, gentleman and scholar

By the time Alfred became king of Wessex, aged bout 22, three elder brothers had already been on the throne. Their fair-minded father Ethelwulf had made the brothers agree to a novel policy of succession by which each surviving brother would in turn take the throne, leaving sufficient property rights to the children of the deceased. Alfred's life as a boy coincided with the great Viking invasion of Britain, hence his accession to the throne at such a tender age.

The early years of his reign were a desperate struggle for survival, and several times he was forced into hiding. It was during this period that the famous legend tells of his stay on

The 'Alfred Jewel'

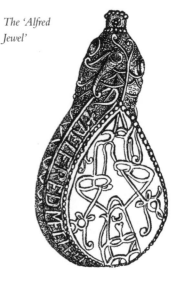

Athelney Island in a swineherd's cottage. After burning the cakes that he was asked to watch Alfred was rebuked by the swineherd's wife, she not knowing he was the king. Yet, from this ignominious position Alfred learned his lesson. Summoning all the strength possessed of his character, he managed, bit by bit, battle by battle, to win back all the territories he had lost.

Making of the man

From an early age Alfred displayed a keen intelligence and an enquiring mind. Before the troubles began, Ethulwulf took Alfred, aged six, on a pilgrimage to Rome where they stayed for over a year. The boy is thought to have received some sort of consecration by the pope, an event which clearly made a lasting impression on him.

Once home, and thrust into the maelstrom of battles, Alfred earned some of his 'greatness' in the way he handled the outcomes. In one of the most important campaigns in English history, at the Battle of Edington in Wiltshire, a prolonged engagement of fierce fighting with heavy swords and axes resulted in victory for the home side and marked a turning point in Wessex's fortunes against the invading hordes.

The manner of Alfred's treatment of his Viking counterpart, Guthrum, was curious. Any one of his Anglo-Saxon predecessors would have slain the enemy there and then. Alfred not only spared Guthrum, but insisted on the pagan becoming baptised as a Christian. Alfred was his godfather.

The Saxon leader's benevolence did not stop there. Alfred then threw a party for the Vikings that lasted many days and showered them with gifts. At the end of the festivities, he released all the captives – and enjoyed peace with them for a decade and a half.

Civilising influence

In peacetime, Alfred did not idle away his days: 'no wise man wants a soft life,' he maintained. Instead he sought to secure his kingdom and subjects as best he could. Knowing that it was only a matter of time before he would have to face more Viking raids, the Saxon king pioneered a fleet of warships, each manned with 60 oars, making them fast in the water. Thus was created England's first navy.

Alfred was also the first English king to devise a rotating system of conscription. Half his subjects would do spells of military service, then return to their usual occupation, while the other half took their place. In this way, Alfred ensured he always had a ready army.

He founded 30 fortified towns, strategically located so that nowhere was more than 20 miles (a day's march) away from another. Each of these settlements, or boroughs (from the Saxon word, burgh, meaning fortress), would have a garrison and land to support the inhabitants, the largest being Winchester, his capital.

The building of these towns gave his subjects a fairer share in society. As opposed to a castle owned by a baron and served by slaves, these boroughs were devised by a Christian mind having due care for his fellow citizens. All would perform to their best ability in support of the whole. In fact Alfred made a survey of his entire kingdom, the 'Book of Winchester', and for the first time divided the land into counties, parishes and hundreds, endeavouring to spread his new model society throughout the land.

Youngest Ever Royal Philanderer
Eadwig the lustful

A lfred the Great's progeny consolidated his gains against the Vikings by restricting them to the Danelaw, an area of Danish self-rule in eastern England between the rivers Thames and Tees. But the Anglo-Saxon success story received a setback when Eadwig, elder son of Edmund I (Alfred's grandson), succeeded to the throne.

Aged only 15, Eadwig was not quite ready to take on the responsibility of ruling the country. Right from the word go, at the coronation ceremony, the new incumbent suddenly vanished from the scene. The abbot of Glastonbury and future English saint, Dunstan, was instructed to find him at once. Trying the royal bedchamber, Dunstan discovered the renegade youth in bed with his fiancée *and* future mother-in-law; his royal accoutrements, including the crown, scattered about the floor.

After such an unpromising start it is no surprise that Eadwig's power waned. Within a few years he had lost the confidence of his allies in Mercia and Northumberland and his rule was restricted to the region south of the Thames. His reign lasted just four years before he died in 959, still a teenager.

Coronation Ceremony is Model for Europe

Edgar 'The Peaceful' is compared to Christ

The account of King Edgar's coronation ceremony at Bath is the first surviving full record of such an occasion in Aengla Land, as the Saxons called it. The Anglo-Saxon Chronicle gives a proud description of its new monarch who is regarded as having an almost messianic quality. Certainly Edgar's reign was seen by posterity as a golden age.

As large crowds gathered at Bath Abbey amid the ruins of Roman Britain, an elaborate coronation ritual was led by Dunstan, brought back from exile by Edgar to be Archbishop of Canterbury. In an unprecedented atmosphere of majestic solemnity, Edgar was heralded as a type of saviour lord of the nation. The account likens the new king to

Coronation liturgy in Anglo-Saxon

Christ, beginning his 'ministry' in his 29th year and being a 'guardian of light'.

The ritual was steeped in religious commitment. Edgar must keep the Church of God and the Christian People in peace, prevent sinfulness in his ranks, and show justice and compassion to all. Then, following a rite of divine ordinance that echoed the precepts of ancient Israel, Edgar was anointed with oil, just as 'Zadok the Priest and Nathan the Prophet anointed Solomon the King'. The regal investiture saw his adornment with sword, rod, sceptre and imperial diadem symbolising Edgar's rule over Britain, Scotland and Ireland. A later piece of political theatre had Edgar ceremonially rowed across the River Dee by sub-kings of his dependent states.

The English coronation was so magnificent that nations right across Europe copied the ceremony for their own purposes. Indeed, the core elements of the service have endured in English coronations down to the present. The same ritual, even the same words, translated from the original Latin, could be heard in Westminster Abbey during the crowning of Elizabeth II in 1953.

Dorset's Great Royal Pilgrimage
Edward the Martyr is champion of Russian Orthodox Church

Edward's father, Edgar of Wessex, may have been a devout king full of intentions to spread peace throughout his kingdom but having three wives only asked for trouble. Three years after Edward's reign

had begun in 975, he was invited to visit his stepmother, Elfreda, at Corfe Castle on the Isle of Purbeck in Dorset. Her motive was not honourable, for she secretly had designs to put her own son, Ethelred (later known as 'the Unready'), on the throne.

The story goes that on returning from a hunt, Edward leaned forward from his horse to take a drink from a cup proffered by the wicked Elfreda. Meanwhile 'the dagger of an attendant pierced him through'. He

clapped spurs to his horse but half fell and, with one foot caught in a stirrup, was dragged through the wood, trailing his blood as he went. Alas, the end of Edward meant the succession of Ethelred.

The political background to this deed was monastic reform, the hot potato of the time. Edward belonged to St Dunstan's stable which wished to reform the monasteries along stricter Benedictine lines. But this was opposed by the rival Mercian kingdom who formed an alliance with Elfreda and supported the accession of Ethelred.

Though the king's earthly life was short (lasting only about 15 years), soon after his death miracles were reported in his name and he became known as Edward the Martyr. Indeed his fame spread far and wide. Pilgrims came to seek his tomb, but his rather plain burial in Wareham was thought to be unworthy.

His body was therefore exhumed and translated by archbishop Dunstan to Shaftesbury Abbey, a distance of 25 miles. A solemn procession took place on foot, during which more miracles were said to have occurred. Seven

days later the charmed bones arrived at their destination. It was probably the greatest religious procession ever to happen in Dorset.

Edward the Martyr's relics might have vanished by the modern era had not the Russian Orthodox Church stepped in to receive them in the 1980s. Believing that the 'old church' doctrine espoused by Dunstan of Glastonbury and Edward the Martyr was close in style and content to their own (for this predates the Great Schism of the 11th century when the Christian Church split into Roman Catholic and Eastern Orthodox), the eastern Church set up a shrine dedicated to Edward at a chapel in Brookwood, Surrey, where they continue to celebrate services in his honour.

Was Ethelred Really 'Unready'?

How come such a sloth reigned for 38 years?

No English king has had a worse press than Ethelred the 'Unready'. Even Richard III and bad King John had their reprieves, but Ethelred has had more disparaging rhymes written about him than any other monarch. Writing a century after his death, William of Malmesbury said of him:

The king, eager and admirably fitted for sleeping, put off such great matters (that is, opposing the Danes) and yawned, and if ever he recovered his senses enough to raise himself upon his elbow, he immediately relapsed into his wretchedness.

But what did Ethelred do to earn such a reputation? Can a man who reigned for 38 years have been all that bad? His great calumny was to give up, not even to try to defend, all that his ancestor Alfred the Great had painstakingly secured from the Vikings nearly two centuries before.

The Anglo-Saxon empire was by the 980s an evidently prosperous state, one of the wealthiest in Europe, with rich pickings to be had if its borders were not well defended. *The Anglo-Saxon Chronicle* tells of a government in disarray, of indecision, treachery, ineptitude, even cruelty, of which Ethelred was the chief culprit.

Facing wave upon wave of Viking invasion, the king became ever more desperate. For a long time Danes had been settled under the Danelaw in eastern parts of the country. In a pique of paranoia, Ethelred issued a decree in 1002 that all Danes be massacred, on the grounds that they wished to depose him. Furthermore this order of execution was extended to all members of his governing counsel, the Witan. Ethelred's nickname, the 'Unready', is a twelfth century translation of the Anglo-Saxon word 'Unraed', meaning 'ill-advised', or 'having no counsel', and may originate from this event, known as the 'Massacre of St Brice's Day'.

THE WITAN: A PROTO-PARLIAMENT

Perhaps the earliest form of English parliament existed in royal Wessex. A body of the king's counsellors, both lay and ecclesiastical, numbering about 100, would meet regularly in what was known as the Witan to debate issues of the day. However, solutions to problems were rarely achieved. Taxes rose to high levels and just as today there were plenty of scandals.

There may well be some exaggeration in this account, but it nevertheless shows the degree of madness that had taken hold of Ethelred's mind. The king, intent at all costs on looking after number one, would ensure he and his family retreated to a safe distance from the flare of battle. One rare instance of initiative amid all the carnage was Ethelred's decision to marry again, this time a Norman noblewoman, named Emma.

The move turned out to be politically expedient. By this time the north of France had been granted to the 'Northmen', hence the name Normandy, and they were using these shores to launch raids on the south coast of England. In marrying Emma, Ethelred could apply enough pressure to stop this and also find a useful ally in times of refuge. When, after 1013, the invasion force under Swein Forkbeard ruthlessly destroyed one city after another, including even the capital Winchester and London, the English king, Emma and their two sons (one of whom was the future Edward the Confessor) fled into exile in Normandy.

Now, as has happened on other occasions of peril, England were rescued by the weather. Their harsh winter of 1014 did for Forkbeard, and while the Danes were busy readying Canute to take his place, the English sent for their king in exile.

His pride puffed up, Ethelred duly consented, though was obliged to accept certain restraints if he were to sit upon the throne again. No longer would he extort high taxes from his subjects, or enslave them. Indeed he should govern in the caring manner of his illustrious predecessors in good Anglo-Saxon spirit. The terms of the agreement were formally written down and enshrined in *The Anglo-Saxon Chronicle*. This 'treaty' represented the first constitutional settlement in England between king and his people. It anticipates the Magna Carta of some 200 years later, and even the Reform Acts of the 19th century.

With a resolve hitherto unknown, Ethelred set about forcing back the Danes, albeit briefly. This time he had along side him the strength and military nous of his now full grown son and heir, Edmund 'Ironside'.

Ironside on the Case
Wessex's pride restored

Edmund II, nicknamed Ironside 'for his valour', had a considerable task before him on taking over the crown from his weak father, Ethelred II. Though the nation had expressed its forgiveness of their errant king when he vowed to fight the Danes, Ethelred's backsliding and death soon afterwards left a divided country for Edmund to rule.

Indeed Ethelred's reign had caused such deep resentments that a powerful lobby, voiced by the bishops of Wessex, opposed Edmund's kingship and instead wished to make the Danish Canute their king: 'They repudiated and renounced in his [Canute's] presence all the race of Ethelred, and concluded peace with him, swearing loyalty to him.'

Edmund had inherited a nation at war with itself. Canute drew on supporters in the north and east to besiege Edmund's stronghold in London, while Edmund rallied as many of his countrymen to his side, especially from his ancestral Wessex. In one campaign after another

Edmund was victorious. After 30-odd years of humiliation, here at last was an Anglo-Saxon king behind whom the nation could unite.

Alas some wounds would never heal. In what was probably a treacherous plot, one Eadric of Mercia joined forces with Edmund when the going suited, only to revert to his alliance with Canute at a critical stage in the Battle of Ashingdon, near Southend. Such double-dealing was, in fact, quite commonplace in Ethelred's time but it was a decisive blow for Edmund's cause – 'all the flower of England perished there'.

However, Edmund survived the battle. Later, while in retreat in Gloucestershire, Canute caught up with him and curiously the two warriors – perhaps out of mutual respect, perhaps for political expediency, but perhaps with skulduggery in mind – agreed to a truce. Indeed they swore to be brothers, exchanged garments, weapons, even gifts. Then they agreed to partition the nation, Canute ruling the north, Edmund the south. An Anglo-Saxon church survives at

Deerhurst where this pact was made. But within a month Edmund was dead, just 23 years old, and Canute was king.

Canute Demonstrates Limits to Earthly Power
England's fiery Danish king is a man of contrasts

Canute is credited with being a great king, of both his Danish territory and England. He did indeed rule for nearly 20 years. But he came to the English throne with a bloody past behind him, for as *The Anglo-Saxon Chronicle* reported at the decisive Battle of Ashingdon,

'Cnut had the victory, though all England fought against him....'

Canute had to pick up several pieces if he was to win over his new client nation.

The Danish king is remembered for the many good things he achieved: restoring peace and stability, and upholding Christian principles. But to do so would be to whitewash his character.

After Edmund Ironside had routed Canute and his army, the Viking king, on his retreat to Denmark, committed one of the most infamous acts of barbarity on record. He disposed of his English hostages by cutting off their hands, ears and noses – hardly acts of a Christian conscience. His ruthless cruelty was also manifest later when back in England seeking absolute power, when he systematically eliminated all potential sources of opposition.

Once Canute had secured the throne in 1016, he imposed a huge one-off tax on his subjects of £70,000 to pay off his Viking army and fleet, so they could return to their homeland on a good pension. This did at least become the final Danegeld the English had to finance. Nevertheless it was crippling to the treasury.

THE DANEGELD
The Danegeld was land tax, agreed by

the English king to pay off Viking invaders. The idea was to persuade them to leave for good, but all it did in practice was entice them back for more, like wild animals returning to a known source of food. With each raid, the sums extracted became greater: £10,000 in 991; £16,000 in 994; £24,000 in 1002; and £30,000 in 1007. The poet Rudyard Kipling summed up the issue:

It is always a temptation for a rich and lazy nation
To puff and look important and to say: –
'Though we know we should defeat you, we have not the time to meet you.
We will therefore pay you cash to go away.'
And that is called paying the Dane-geld;
But we've proved it again and again, That if once you have paid him the Dane-geld
You never get rid of the Dane.'
(Rudyard Kipling, 'Dane-Geld', 1911)

Thereafter the new king seems to have set about transforming his image into a more benevolent, if tough, leader. Very likely the Catholic Church, through the work of Archbishop Wulfstan, had a hand in this process. In what seems to have been a bid to reconcile himself to the English people, Canute married Ethelred's widow, Emma of Normandy. Together they planned a series of religious ceremonies designed to lay the ghost of the past.

They underwent a pilgrimage of sorts to Ashingdon where Canute 'ordered to be built a minster of stone and lime for the souls of the men who were there slain.' In another act of reconciliation, they humbly translated to Canterbury the relics of St Aelfheah, archbishop of Canterbury, who had been brutally butchered to death by drunken Danish louts during the war years.

Finally, in an attempt to raise himself to the exalted House of Wessex, the king, with the help of his queen, ceremonially presented a magnificent gold cross to the New Minster at Winchester, traditional capital of Saxon England.

Canute tried his very hardest to portray himself as a bona fide English king. Yet he made no attempt, when the opportunity was there, to rise above his station. Unlike his Saxon predecessors, he claimed no divine authority. To make this abundantly clear he gave his famous demonstration on the beach.

His courtiers had claimed, perhaps sycophantically, that Canute was so great that even nature would obey him. The king ordered his throne to be carried down to the water's edge, whereupon he sat on it and ordered the sea to recede. Contrary to popular understanding of the legend, Canute was not trying to prove that he had power over the waves. He sat there as the waves lapped over his feet. Finally, shin deep in water, Canute announced, 'Let it be known that the power of kings is empty and worthless compared with the majesty of God.' This was now the Christian king, having once been a marauding Viking terrorist, whom the English had recast as their own.

Saintly Healer of the King's Evil
But was the founder of Westminster Abbey really that pious?

The popular image of Edward the Confessor is of a tall white-haired man with a long aristocratic face. This noble demeanour certainly served future monks well in reinforcing the idea that this Englishman was a pious, almost ascetic, king whose marriage was reputedly celibate on the grounds of

chastity. Hence no heir.

Edward's later canonisation, based largely on his apparent ability to heal scrofula (a form of tuberculosis of the neck) by touching the sufferer, led to his enormous popularity in the Middle Ages when pilgrims in their droves would visit his shrine in Westminster Abbey in the hope of being cured of their illnesses. This charismatic gift was perceived to come from the king's divine authority, hence scrofula's alternative name as the 'King's Evil'. If he could cure an individual, the logic ran, he could protect the nation; and so for 400 years Edward rode high as the patron saint of England.

But was he all that religious really? The question arises because of other known facts about him. His everyday life was much as one would expect of a king at this time. He loved hunting, 'delighting at the baying and scrambling of hounds', enjoyed listening to bloody-thirsty Norse sagas in the evening, and did not shirk battle duty when required. By all accounts he was a red-blooded male, not otherworldly, as his icon suggests.

Marriage problems

His marriage to Edith, the domineering daughter of Godwin, earl of Wessex, had its difficulties. Edward became increasingly suspicious of his father-in-law's political motives and eventually they came to arms. In the end Edith became her husband's open enemy. All her property was confiscated and she was sent to a nunnery.

Is it not perfectly possible that Edward and Edith simply failed to conceive a child, or that the union was loveless? Perhaps later church figures embellished the virtue of Edward in order to justify, and promote further, his popularity.

With his background as it was – his mother Emma was Norman, and he was brought up in Normandy where his Saxon father Ethelred lived in exile – you might think he favoured the French as much as the English. He may never have wished for the likes of Godwin (whose son would accede as Harold II) to take the English throne. So it was no wonder that Edward secretly promised the crown to his Norman nephew William, who of course would soon invade to take what he considered rightfully his.

Westminster Abbey

The building of Westminster Abbey must go down as Edward's major triumph. It easily became the largest church in England and one of the finest in western Europe. Again his inspiration no doubt came from France where, as a boy, he would have seen other cathedrals being built in the grand new Romanesque style.

So why did Edward choose this difficult spot on Thorney Island surrounded by marshland when his dynastic roots lay in Winchester? He may well have been inspired by the tale that the ground was made holy by St Peter, but the real reason lies in its proximity to the City of London.

Though the city had long been the commercial capital, it was here that Edward had fought Godwin in the decisive battles of his campaign against the troublesome earl. Here was the place of his victory and here should be his political capital.

Thus it was in 1050 that Edward the Confessor moved his court to what became called the Palace of Westminster, a name retained to this day as the home of Parliament.

Portents of Disaster
Shipwreck and shooting star spell the end of Saxon England

On his deathbed in January 1066, Edward the Confessor had a dream that God's curse lay on England for her sins. With unseemly haste Earl Godwin's son, Harold, took the throne with the blessing of his Saxon peers before either of his rival pretenders, Edgar the Atheling or Hardrada, king of Norway, could press their claims. Though Harold had served Edward faithfully for many years as his military commander, many believed his enthronement in Westminster Abbey – literally within hours of the outgoing king's burial – would disturb Providence. There was also William, Duke of Normandy, to consider. Had not Edward the

Confessor strangely promised him the English crown?

Another promise, however, carried yet more weight. Two years earlier, Harold had embarked on a trip into the English Channel, a journey that has prompted a good deal of speculation. He departed from Bosham on the south coast, allegedly after a merry feast. The depiction of Harold in the Bayeux Tapestry shows him carrying a hawk and a hound in a single boat, suggesting merely a pleasure trip.

French trick?

The French version of events says that Harold had been instructed by the English king to go to Normandy and swear allegiance to William. Well, it would, wouldn't it? Whatever the motive, Harold's expedition ran into stormy weather, he was shipwrecked off the coast of Normandy and arrested by Count Guy of Ponthieu. The Norman account continues with the hapless Harold being rescued by Duke William and in return Harold helps him fight his enemies in Brittany. For his great valour Harold is honoured with a knighthood, and

at some stage he apparently swears an oath of fealty to William.

Unfortunately there is no record in *The Anglo-Saxon Chronicle* to confirm or deny this account, nor to clarify exactly what French status Harold was supporting. Doesn't it seem strange that Harold, who had every reason to think he himself to be the next English king, should give away the crown so lightly? Unless, perhaps, he was tricked in some way.

Certainly he must have been under extreme pressure in the circumstances, for he was in William's power. All the Norman nobles, knights, and churchmen crowded round him bearing witness to the deed. Once the oath had been sworn, it seems William stood up from his ducal throne, and stepped forward to remove a cloth revealing a special casket containing holy relics. The significance is obscure but may it not be possible that Harold believed he was simply endorsing William's claim to some French seat of power, not the English throne, and that this promise bore unbreakable divine sanction? Perhaps Harold was confused and simply went along with events to show good faith.

At any rate, his return to England was received badly. The Bayeux Tapestry depicts Edward pointing an accusatory finger at Harold. Had the king perhaps just got wind of the fact that his commander had just given away his kingdom? These circumstances might explain the hastiness with which Harold had himself crowned.

Heavenly portent

An anxious public feared that all may not be well in the heavenly abode. As Harold appeared at Easter tide donning the crown, some shivers of apprehension must have greeted him. And sure enough, their misgivings were justified. Within weeks, a startling apparition appeared in the sky. The shape of a gigantic flaming sword burned the eyes of its beholders. For seven nights it blazed forth. There was no doubt God was expressing his disapproval. And the symbol of his choice could mean only one thing: disaster for the Saxon kingdom.

Not realising that this celestial event was in fact a periodic manifestation of Halley's Comet, the English people feared the worst. And indeed, despite Harold's heroic efforts to repel invasions on two fronts – first from the Scandinavian Hardrada in York, and then from William of Normandy at Hastings – the providential sign proved to be true. As *The Anglo-Saxon Chronicle* declared, 'the Frenchmen gained the field of battle, as God granted them for the sins of the nation.' Thus began the Norman Conquest which would change the culture of England forever.

Changed Forever
William the Conqueror ensures no reversions

It is often assumed that once William of Normandy had won the Battle of Hastings in 1066 and killed King Harold the rest of the country was a pushover. In fact, it took him seven gruelling long years of battle before he gained complete control.

After Hastings, William had no more than a foot in the door of England. There were too many other interested parties for the conquest to be straightforward. Besides, his army

was limited in numbers to how many could be shipped across the Channel at any one time. He attacked London with only about 7000 men and had to rely on strategy and cunning. His terror tactics worked on the English people's low morale, feeling as they did that the Normans were instruments of God's vengeance.

Nevertheless, as William would find out, there were many pockets of fierce Saxon resistance, determined not relinquish their land without a fight - the rebellion led by Hereward the Wake in East Anglia was particularly ferocious. And William had to contend with Danish incursions too. But the Conqueror was tough and cruel. He would think nothing of destroying whatever might stand in his way, if necessary slaughtering livestock, smashing crops, even burning whole Saxon villages.

The feudal system

The only way William could hope to secure a lasting stranglehold on his new kingdom was to build castles everywhere, and so he did in virtually every main town of Britain. The largest strongholds were the Tower of London and Windsor Castle.

Nothing of the like had been seen before in Anglo-Saxon England. Alfred the great had built fortified towns, the burghs, designed to protect the inhabitants from Danish raids. But the new Norman model of the motte and bailey – a wooden, pallisaded keep towering over a fortified compound – stood out mightily in the landscape, a constant reminder of the brute force of the new regime. Norman feudalism was born: a two-tier society now operated of Norman lords and Anglo-Saxon underlings.

Symbols of Norman power

As a master, indeed an obsessive, of law and order, William ordered an exhaustive inventory to be drawn up itemising every building in the land. This became known as the Domesday Book (from the Latin *domus*, 'home'). In so doing William could ensure that every burgh had a baron registered in charge who could be summoned to meetings at which new legislation could be delivered. Old Sarum, whose ruins can be seen above Salisbury Plain, was the site of his great court.

William the Conqueror's building programme was unparalleled in Europe. As well as castles, he built numerous cathedrals. Thus came to Britain the Norman style of church architecture, with its massive stone columns and wide naves, which in themselves stood out as awesome symbols of the permanence of the Conquest.

At Winchester William ordered the construction of a much greater cathedral than the existing Old Minster to demonstrate how much more powerful was his earthly rule than that of his Saxon predecessors. And just to ram home the point, he had himself re-crowned every Easter in the Old Minster while the works were going on next door.

William also had the area around Winchester cleared to create a royal hunting ground, known as the New Forest. Deer and boar became protected species in this and many other royal reserves created. Poaching was made a capital offence.

As a measure of the man's stamina, William was still Duke of Normandy and so had to maintain his duties there too. Constantly needing to tear off to France to fix some squabble or other, the new king of England must have spent a good deal of his life on horseback.

The activity must have helped to keep him fit and healthy for William lived into his sixties – not bad for a man of this time. Although dying lonely and sad, he passed on to his offspring a kingdom which, in spite of everything, became a peaceable land. It was said that 'a man might go the length and breadth of the kingdom with his pockets full of gold … and no man durst slay another'; one might add, 'for fear of the law'!

Live by the Arrow and Ye Shall Die by the Arrow

William 'Rufus' gets his comeuppance

On his deathbed William the Conqueror, in typically organised fashion, made plans for the division of his territories. His eldest son, Robert, would inherit Normandy, William 'Rufus' (so named for his ruddy features and flaxen hair), would get all England, and the youngest, Henry (future Henry I), would be given a modest sum of money.

His namesake, though the favourite son, proved to be quite a different character. Savage and ruthless he was, like his father, but much more wayward, unpredictable, and, above all, dishonourable.

William II had little respect for anyone – for his subjects, even for his fellow noblemen, and certainly very little for the Church. When the see of Canterbury fell vacant after the death of Archbishop Lanfranc, William refused to fill the post for four years, instead siphoning off its funds for his own pleasure. When the no-nonsense scholar Anselm was sent by the pope to fill the position, he soon fell out with William over the matter and was rapidly forced into exile.

Unfair sport

It was in the field of recreational sport that the people of England, the Anglo-Saxons, felt the hurt most.

William Rufus continued the policy of his father of turning land over to hunting reserves. Both the poor and the rich were affected. Cultivated land as well as rough pasture was confiscated, so the poor suddenly found they were without a food supply, while the rich could not indulge in their traditional sport. The unpopularity of this policy resulted in a growing restlessness in the country and when Rufus found one day he had a rebellion from his own nobles on his hands, he was made to think hard about his options.

Rather than come to terms with his fellow French speakers, Rufus turned to his Anglo-Saxon subjects for support:

He then sent after Englishmen, described to them his need, earnestly requested their support, and promised them the best laws that ever before were in this land; each unright guild [geld, or tax] he forbade and restored to the men their woods and chases. (The Anglo-Saxon Chronicle, 1088)

The promise of their hunting rights restored, people volunteered their military services and Rufus could quell the uprising at Rochester. Alas, once the matter was resolved, it was business as usual; the promised reform was quietly forgotten.

Shot by arrow

The story about the death of Rufus is well known but we do not know whether it happened by accident or was an assassination. One afternoon in August William led a hunting party in the New Forest near Brockenhurst. His brother Henry was with him. One of the huntsmen, Walter Tyrell, was supposedly aiming at a stag but his arrow instead struck the king, who died instantly. The party was thrown into a panic and fled the scene.

The king's body was later found by a charcoal-burner, named Purkiss, who took the corpse on a cart to Winchester. In a flurry of anxiety the king was quickly buried beneath the cathedral tower with no rites. Henry ransacked the treasury and had himself crowned, while Tyrell fled abroad never to return.

As though by act of divine displeasure at these proceedings, the tower collapsed two years later, confirming suspicions that an ill deed was committed in those woods. Did Henry and his counsellors run the risk that the king's deep unpopularity would allow them to get away with this 'accident', thus enabling Henry to snatch the crown while his elder brother, and rightful heir, Robert was absent on crusade?

The King Never Smiled Again
The sorrowful fate of Henry I

On the death of his brother William Rufus in 1100, Henry illegally took the throne of England ahead of his second-eldest brother, Robert Curthose. His excuse may well have been that Robert was away on crusading duty in the Holy Land.

Indeed Robert had been offered the kingship of Jerusalem. But Henry knew that it was only a matter of time before his brother would be back challenging him for what he believed to be his rightful inheritance.

Luckily Henry was proving popular with the people. He took the politically expedient measures of repealing Rufus's hated laws on hunting restrictions and of recalling Anselm from exile to resume his position as Archbishop of Canterbury.

The shrewdest move, however, was to marry Edith of Scotland. She was daughter of Malcolm III and, more important still, was descended from Alfred the Great. Thereby the union restored the ancient royal House of Wessex to the English throne, a highly popular outcome with his Saxon subjects. Henry stood in good stead to receive his brother.

And so to arms

On his eventual arrival at Portsmouth, with a massed army at his side, Robert marched to Alton in Hampshire where he duly met Henry. In a unique confrontation the two opposing forces formed a circle, while the brothers met in the middle. After a few tense minutes of negotiation, they threw their arms round each other in an extraordinary gesture of reconciliation. All seemed well, but Robert clearly became disgruntled and eventually the brothers did come to blows, in Normandy. Victorious Henry locked up Robert for life and sequestered his dukedom. So it was, on the 40th anniversary of the Battle of Hastings, that history reversed itself: the English had conquered Normandy.

Once again all seemed well. Henry and his wife, now renamed as the fashionably Norman Matilda to keep his nobles happy, had four children, of which two were sons and potential heirs. He is also credited with fathering at least 20 illegitimate children, a record in royal annals.

But the king's lusty happiness was not destined to last. One legitimate son died young; the other, William Aethling (named after his Anglo-Saxon ancestor), died tragically at sea. He was returning after dark to England from Normandy aboard *The White Ship* on its maiden voyage, when the vessel struck a rock and sank. On hearing of the tragedy from the sole survivor, Henry is said to have been so devastated that he never smiled again.

Desperate to have another male heir, the king married again at the age of 53: this time to a French girl of 18.

But no son was forthcoming. Instead he resolved to prepare his daughter, also called Matilda, for succession. Henry I reigned for 35 years.

Twelve Year Old Weds Holy Roman Emperor
Uncrowned Queen Matilda mothers Plantagenet dynasty

Although Matilda was never actually crowned queen of England, she was effectively the queen in the sense of being ruler of the nation. This 'reign' lasted only a few months in 1141, and it proved a considerable struggle.

Matilda was made of stern stuff with great will power. Daughter of Henry I and Matilda of Scotland, she was promised the throne by her father, since his only rightful male heir had died in an accident at sea.

Her ambitious father managed to present his daughter in all the right circles, and at the tender age of twelve she was married to Henry V, Holy Roman Emperor, no less. She had to learn German fast and lived in Germany. As a result of this union she is often referred to as

Empress Matilda. After ten years of marriage, however, the emperor died. Her forever networking father then arranged a second marriage for her, this time to Geoffrey Plantagenet, son of the Count of Anjou. An erstwhile enemy was thereby befriended and, of course, the foundations were laid for the Plantagenet empire ruled by the future Henry II.

All Matilda had to do was grasp the reins of power. And this would occupy her energies for a good deal of her remaining life. Her rival to the throne would be Stephen, grandson of William the Conqueror through his daughter Adela.

Although Stephen had been made to swear an oath supporting Matilda's succession to the throne, he had other ideas when Henry I died. Commanding more support than Matilda could muster from nobles and bishops, Stephen was able to seize the throne. There was little that Matilda could do to dislodge the usurper, until he foolishly placed himself in a vulnerable position.

During a skirmish in Lincoln he climbed down from his horse and continued fighting on the ground.

When his weapons broke, the king fell to the mercy of Matilda's knights who clapped him in prison.

Thereupon Matilda endeavoured to persuade the aristocracy to grant this woman her rightful status. However, the former empress's haughty demeanour made her more enemies than friends, and on rejecting demands to halve her subjects' tax bill, she was refused the coronation. Instead her main ally, the powerful bishop Henry of Blois conferred on her the tentative title of 'Domina', or 'Lady of the English'.

But this state of affairs was never going to last and within a couple of months the country was in a state of civil war. One day, while residing at home in Winchester, she discovered that fire was enveloping the town – and no accident either. For several weeks the city was ablaze, the great abbey was destroyed and with it a great gold cross given by King Canute. When the army of her former ally, turned enemy, Bishop Henry arrived from London, Matilda's supporters fled. She herself escaped but Stephen was released from prison and was soon hunting her down.

Bitter years of siege and counter-siege followed, including once when encircled at Oxford Matilda managed to escape by crossing the snow-laden land wearing a white cape as camouflage. Eventually the two adversaries came to a settlement: Stephen would keep the crown if Matilda's son Henry (by Geoffrey Planatagenet) could become heir to the throne. And so their conflict ended. In fact, Stephen died a year later so Matilda had the more sastisfactory outcome.

Anarchy under Stephen
Worst excesses in English history

Possibly the most anarchic years the country has witnessed – worse even than during the English Civil War – were those experienced during the reign of Stephen. He himself was by all reports a likeable fellow: good-looking, kindly, generous – hardly the sort to wish for such a dreadful state of affairs. Unfortunately Stephen was not suited to being a king. He was out of his depth.

Descriptions of his reign from contemporary sources beggar belief.

It seems that Stephen's bid to hold on to his crown in the face of the iron-willed Matilda (whose right to the throne had been asserted by her father Henry I) simply got out of hand. Once Stephen had lost control, he was unable to regain it.

Rival factions of nobles and knights fought bitterly, each in turn burning and pillaging whole villages that might have pledged their support to the enemy. A protection racket was rife. It was said that 'you could easily go a day's journey without ever finding a village inhabited or a field cultivated.'

Even those who escaped the wholesale slaughter would probably suffer in the following famine that overtook much of the land. William of Malmesbury recorded, 'The knights from the castles carried off both herds and flocks ... pillaging the dwellings of the wretched countrymen to the very straw.' Entire towns, such as Nottingham, Winchester, Oxford, Cambridge and Bedford were sacked, and thousands starved to death in the famine. It was said that every man who could, robbed his neighbour. Unspeakable tortures were committed to obtain treasures. Bodies were 'broken on stones' and the worst perpetrators 'knotted cords round their heads and twisted them till they entered the brain'.

We do not know how much licence was written into these accounts, perhaps none. Such lawless horror prevailed for 15 years under Stephen's reign. It took the strength and organisation skills of his successor, Henry II, to put an end to the chaos.

Penitent Ruler of Europe's Largest Empire
Henry II and his 'turbulent priest'

Winston Churchill's eponymous ancestor acclaimed the first Plantagenet ruler, Henry II, as the 'very greatest King that England ever knew, but withal the most unfortunate'.

By his birth to Matilda and her second husband, Geoffrey of Anjou, Henry inherited the English crown. Through his marriage to Eleanor of Aquitaine, he acquired half of France, and bit by bit during his reign Henry added virtually the rest of the country. He conquered Ireland too. So by

1180 this formidable warrior king had extended the frontiers of what could rightly be termed the Angevin Empire to include an immense area stretching from the Scottish border to the Pyrenees.

In his efforts to quell the turmoil inherited on succeeding Stephen, Henry earned widespread support from his nobles. One measure was to introduce a system of common law that standardized legal practice right across the country. Thus far, the history books present Henry II in a good light. But the second part of Churchill's statement refers to his less successful dealings with the Church.

Henry did not like sharing power with another institution, especially one that regarded itself as having supreme authority.

Yet his reign started well on this front. When Henry was introduced to the brilliant young Thomas Becket, a protégé of Archbishop Theobald of Canterbury, they immediately saw eye to eye and Henry made him royal chancellor. As soon as the Canterbury post fell vacant, the king fast-tracked his learned friend through the ordination process, from priest to bishop to archbishop, in a matter of days. Unfortunately, from there on their paths diverged.

Parting of ways

As Becket himself declared on taking up his new position, he changed from 'a patron of play-actors and a follower of hounds, to being a shepherd of souls.' The two friends disagreed on several points of ecclesiastical administration as Henry endeavoured to assert the secular law over church law. Becket constantly refused to oblige.

Uppermost was the issue of jurisdiction over clergymen convicted of crimes. Henry wanted control of their sentencing and reprieve. Becket insisted it was a matter for the Church. Although this may not in itself seem to be a matter of life and death, the verdict would symbolize where the power lay.

In effect the two men were drawing up their battle lines – to give ground here would only lead to conceding more territory later. Like Thomas More centuries later in his resistance to Henry VIII, Becket could not act against his conscience, or all would be lost.

At one point Becket felt so intimidated he fled to France where he stayed for six years until Henry allowed him back after the Pope had threatened to excommunicate the whole of Britain. Here, indeed, were the early rumblings of the split that eventually ripped the English Church from Rome in the 16th century.

Final solution

When Becket preached with characteristic fire on Christmas Day, excommunicating bishops who had taken part in the coronation of Henry's son as future king, the report of it tipped Henry into the terrible rage that would haunt him for the rest of his life. His actual words – 'What miserable drones and traitors have I nurtured and promoted in my household who let their lord be treated with such shameful contempt by a low-born cleric!' – have been turned into the more theatrically terse: 'Who will rid me of this turbulent priest?'

Did the king know that four of his trusty, though not the brightest, barons were within earshot? Did he intend this outburst to be effectively an order of execution? Surely the original words could not be construed to carry that meaning, but the re-rendering of them in a more snesational style surely could.

What we do know is that once the king heard of the murderous deed, committed, as it was, before the high altar of Canterbury Cathedral he was horrified and abject with remorse. In an act of penitence he donned sackcloth and ashes and ate nothing for three days. Four years later, after the pope had canonised Becket, Henry made a public confession of humility and sorrow by walking in sackcloth barefoot to the cathedral and staying overnight in a dank cell of the crypt. Never had such a loose utterance caused such distress to an English monarch.

REBELLIOUS SONS

Early in the 1170s Henry II was at his most powerful. The threat to his empire came not from abroad but from his very own sons, aided by their influential mother Eleanor of Aquitaine. To their chagrin Henry took the unprecedented step of anointing his eldest son Henry as future king of England. In all of English history, this has happened only once during the king's lifetime. But the Young King died in 1183, and a few years later another son, Geoffrey, also died. Richard (the Lionheart) and John were now direct rivals to the throne. Richard courted favour from Philip II of France, who was determined to undo the Angevin Empire. Between them they forced the ageing Henry to accept a humiliating truce and Richard took the throne in 1189 on the king's death.

Ransom for a King
Chivalrous 'Lionheart' who cost his country dear

Probably his upbringing in Poitiers at his mother's court sowed the seeds of Richard's love affair with chivalric combat. Every day he would take part in jousting tournaments and receive expert training in the art of war. No wonder his heart was inflamed with the romance of medieval battle.

So was born England's brave knightly king, dubbed Coeur de Lion, or 'Lionheart'. His love of fighting was such that in the ten years of his reign (1189-99) only a few months were ever spent in England.

MASSACRE AT BANQUET

A magnificent coronation banquet in Westminster was intended to celebrate the new kingship of Richard I. However, trouble started when Jewish leaders tried to pay their respects. A royal decree had forbidden their presence and the group was bundled out. Some of them were beaten, others killed, and anti-Semitic rioting spread through the capital. Richard was anxious to quell the unrest, particularly as he was hoping to raise funds for his crusade from Jewish money-lenders. Sporadic outbreaks of violence towards Jews continued, with a particularly gruesome incident in York the following year.

Richard I and Saladin in combat

On crusade

Richard's greatest endeavour was leading the Third Crusade. On hearing the news that Saladin had invaded the Holy Land, Richard was champing at the bit to take the cross.

Within months of being crowned king, Lionheart was laying plans to rescue the Holy Land from the Muslim infidel. The 'Saladin Tithe' was raised to fund the expedition. Those who joined the crusade would be exempt from the tax which demanded ten per cent of all revenues.

Allied with Philip II of France, his friend and possible lover, the two kings led a huge army across Europe in the summer of 1190. Two interludes delayed the expedition: while overwintering in Sicily Richard's mother arrived and presented him with a bride, Berengaria of Navarre. This match angered Philip who thought Richard should marry his sister Alice, and the two friends fell out. After capturing Cyprus Richard satisfied his mother's demand and married Berengaria.

Cyprus would serve as a base for supplying future crusaders. Richard took his new queen with him to the Holy Land where she witnessed his conquest of Acre and Jaffa. The army then turned inland and headed for the dream goal of their cause, Jerusalem.

Harassed all the way by Saladin's army, the crusaders got within sight of the Holy City. But then Richard received news that his brother John had joined forces with his former friend King Philip and the two were taking control of Normandy castles.

As the situation worsened by the day Richard was forced to make peace with Saladin, having spent 15 months in Palestine. The outcome was deeply frustrating for the English king, for without recapturing Jerusalem the crusade was technically a failure. Nevertheless much of the expedition had been a success: he had recovered the coastal strip; the political turmoil in Jerusalem was resolved; and Christians and Saracens were allowed safe passage to and from the Holy Sepulchre.

A price to pay

Having sent his wife on before him, Richard travelled back to western Europe. He was shipwrecked near

Venice and is said to have made his way on foot disguised as a pilgrim. The king was spotted, however, and taken prisoner by the Duke of Austria. He passed Richard to Henry VI, Holy Roman Emperor, who saw a neat opportunity to raise much needed war funds.

The emperor ransomed Richard for 150,000 marks, a sum greater than the entire Saladin Tithe raised to finance the Third Crusade. To release Richard, the English people, who had hardly ever seen their king, were asked to stump up a quarter of the value of their property. In their scheming ways, John and Philip of France even offered the German Emperor a sum to keep Richard locked up, but it was turned down.

Fortunately for Richard, England prospered from its thriving wool industry and he regained his freedom. But happiness proved shortlived. On his return he discovered a whole swathe of Normandy and Touraine had been taken by John and Philip.

Painstakingly he devoted the last five years of his reign struggling to recover lost land. But this he did. By the time he died, from a crossbow bolt to the shoulder which turned gangrenous, Richard had restored much of his dominion.

Church Bells Fall Silent
King John invokes the wrath of all

The unexpected death of Richard I led to great confusion in courtly circles about his succession. There were two rival candidates: Richard's brother John and Arthur of Brittany, grandson of Henry II.

When the news broke, John was actually staying with Arthur in Brittany. In a tense situation John politely made his adieus and hastened to London to claim his crown.

A nervous character, John had an unfortunate upbringing. His mother, Eleanor of Aquitaine, was 45 when she bore him, the last of eight children and probably unwanted. Soon after his birth Eleanor was placed under house arrest and his brothers despised him. He also inherited no territory, and was nicknamed 'Lackland' for the humiliation. Unsurprisingly, John became a vengeful person, known to be cruel and untrustworthy – the sort who would grab at any useful opportunity whether right or wrong.

Rival camps voiced their support. The archbishop of Canterbury, Hubert Walter, advised against John's coronation, telling his advisors, 'Mark my words, you will never regret anything in your life as much as this [crowning John]'. But in honour of his father's deathbed wish, John was duly crowned king in 1199. An axis of opposition was thereby created. Whilst England and Normandy accepted John, the provinces of Anjou, Maine and Touraine all sided with Arthur.

John knew he had to dispose of his twelve-year-old nephew at the first opportunity if he was going to rid himself of a powerful rival. This opportunity did not arise for a few years but when it did John seized it with both hands.

Young pretender disappears

While only 16, Arthur mysteriously disappeared. He was captured by John's forces in the Battle of Mirabeau and held in the castle of Falaise. The grandson of Henry II was a hero to the Breton people and his imprisonment caused great anger.

It was reported that John had ordered the royal chamberlain, at whose castle Arthur was held, to blind and castrate the boy, but the deed was never done. Instead the chamberlain announced that the boy had died of a heart attack. But when John realised the chamberlain had been lying, he took matters into his own hands. It is said that after inviting the teenager to dinner, John fell into a drunken state and murdered the boy. The king then personally disposed of the body by hurling it into the River Seine.

Ban on church services

This despicable act set the tone for the rest of John's innings, which went from bad to worse. More and more of his empire was being eroded away in wars with France, and it would not be long before France and England became separate political entities.

Given John's irascible nature, it was perhaps inevitable that he would fall out with the Pope over the issue of who should be the next archbishop at Canterbury. The king's excommunication was followed by a papal 'interdict' banning all church services in England except for burying the dead. No church bells rang in England for six years.

MAGNA CARTA

In May 1215 rebel barons captured London and forced King John, who had retreated to the White Tower, to make peace with France. Having cornered the king, they took the opportunity of making him agree to their terms, which would be enshrined in a charter known as Magna Carta, signed on a meadow at Runnymede in Surrey. The charter essentially safeguarded the privileges of the barons and the church. King John is said to have agreed without even reading the document, simply to buy his freedom.

Too Nice For His Own Good
Civilised Henry III loses touch

Henry III was known to be a cultured monarch. He preferred the arts to war and led his nation into a golden age of church building in the Early Gothic style so popular in northern France. Having inherited a kingdom in disarray at the age of nine – his father John had lost nearly all the overseas possessions of the Angevin Empire; only Gascony and Perigord remained in English hands

– Henry relied on having competent advisors to get his reign off to a good start. Fortunately they were, and the country united behind its promising young monarch.

Immigration problem

Henry endeavoured to form useful political alliances with European leaders, seeing this to be the way to keeping the realm peaceful and happy. But what he did not anticipate was that his marriage to Eleanor of Provence in 1236, coupled with his own endearing charm, encouraged a swarm of foreigners to flood into the country. Relatives and friends of the new queen regarded England as the fashionable land of commercial opportunity now that the Holy Land no longer provided rich pickings for crusaders.

But this mass immigration of French aristocrats did not go down well with Henry's barons who felt their noses put out of joint. Their resentment reached a peak when the king made the eccentric decision to invade Sicily with the intention of giving the land, albeit with the Pope's consent, to his ten-year-old second son, Edmund. When the venture turned into a fiasco, causing huge expense to the treasury, the barons were outraged.

Rule by parliament

Exasperated, the English barons decided enough was enough and would put a stop to Henry's fickle ideas. In 1258 the earl of Leicester and the king's brother-in-law, Simon de Montfort, led a committee of 24 barons to confront the king.

However, their intention was not so much to coerce the king with force, but to persuade him with tact of the better course of government they could recommend. On arriving at Westminster Hall the barons left their swords outside, and while they professed loyalty to the king demanded a prerogative to make reforms to state affairs which, to be frank, were a mess.

Together the barons governed the country for several years. But it was an uneasy arrangement, and culminated in Simon de Montfort doing battle with the king's army in 1264 and capturing both Henry and his young warrior son Edward (future Edward I) at the

Battle of Lewes. A year in precarious power saw de Montfort's baronial support wane and the king's wax. The two forces came head to head at the Battle of Evesham, where the earl of Leicester was slain. King Henry could now reassert his authority.

After the drawn out turbulence of much of his reign Henry was content to hand over the running of the country to his forceful son Edward, while he concentrated his energies on what he loved best: art and architecture (of which his greatest achievement was to rebuild Westminster Abbey).

Henry was 65 when he died and despite the upheavals had held the throne for the longest of any English monarch to date, at 56 years.

ROYAL MENAGERIE

An indication of Henry's eccentric nature was his penchant for collecting exotic animals. The first were two leopards, followed by an elephant, gifted by Louis IX of France – no one in England had ever seen such fine beasts. Though housed in purpose built barns, conditions were cramped, and it is thought they did not fare

well. Luckier was the zoo's other great attraction, a polar bear, which Londoners could see daily hunting fish in the River Thames.

Zealous Reformer Persecutes Minorities
Edward I expels Jews and prostitutes

Nicknamed 'Longshank' for his tall stature, Edward I was hailed as a mighty king – 'Hammer of the Scots' and great castle-builder who famously necklaced Wales with a ring of impregnable forts. One of England's stongest ever kings went far towards unifying Britain under a radical reforming of the law.

It is to Edward that we owe thanks for introducing the Model Parliament, which lay the foundations of the

present English system. The common law courts too developed during his reign. Edward was undoubtedly years ahead of his time in the advances he brought to society. But it must not be forgotten that his rule allowed little toleration. Iron fist, not soft glove, was the order of the day.

One of his infamous blitzes was on public morality. Believing that the citizens of his capital were being corrupted by loose women, Edward banned prostitutes from operating anywhere in the City of London. His decree maintained that 'houses of women of evil life' also encouraged thieving and murder. Prostitutes were forbidden from living within the City

walls, and any contravention would result in 40 days in jail. The net effect, of course, was to drive the business across the Thames to Bankside in Southwark, which lay outside the City's jurisdiction. There, licensed brothels and 'stews' (bath-houses) sprang up everywhere after this measure was introduced.

In a further attempt at 'cleansing' society, Edward infamously issued an edict in 1290 requiring the immediate expulsion of all Jews from England. Outbreaks of anti-Semitism had occurred intermittently over the last century, as stories circulated that Jews committed atrocities. The reality was that their traditional role as money-lenders had run its course. High taxation, enforced loans and property confiscation had left most of the 3000 or so members of the community bankrupt.

CREATION OF THE PRINCE OF WALES

Edward I made the first appointment of the Prince of Wales in 1301 by so naming his son Edward. The position was created partly to present the people of Wales with a royal figure to symbolise their place in the monarchy, and partly to proclaim the heir apparent. The investiture took place at Caernarfon in North Wales.

Old Enemy Vanquished in a Day
Robert 'the Bruce' delivers at Bannockburn

Robert I of Scotland wore two hats: one as servant in the court of the English king Edward I, the other as warrior in the cause of Scottish independence. Whenever a revolt against the English was raised Bruce would join it. After defeat he would swear allegiance again to the English throne.

Once crowned king of Scotland at Scone, however, Bruce never looked back. His commitment to winning

independence from the belligerent Edward, who had overrun most of Scotland, was never in doubt.

But the going proved tough. His compatriots suffered heavily at the hands of the English and Bruce himself was forced into hiding on the island of Rathlin, off the Antrim coast (it is here that the legend says Bruce learned to persevere by watching a spider repeatedly trying to spin its web until it succeeded).

His lands were confiscated, his wife and daughter imprisoned, and three of his brothers were executed. Many captives of the English king had their heads paraded on spikes as a tactic to intimidate the enemy.

In fact this had the opposite effect. When Edward I finally died and his weaker son, Edward II, took the throne, the Scots felt rejuvenated. Everywhere they rallied to Bruce's banner – and nowhere was victory sweeter than at Bannockburn.

Bannockburn
The focus of the clash between the two armies would be Stirling Castle. In the seven years since Edward II became king, the Scots had recovered

virtually all the lands taken by his father. All that remained was this stronghold at Stirling.

Standing high up on a rock overlooking the marshy plain of Bannockburn, the fort guarded the key crossing point of the River Forth. On Midsummer's Day, 1314, an anxious commander in charge of the castle, Sir Philip Mowbray, had struck a bargain with the waiting Scots that he would hand over the fort to them unless the English army appeared before sunset that day.

Just in time Edward appeared on the banks of the Bannock. With him was an immense army of 2,500 professional knights on horseback and 15,000 infantry. Mowbray rode out to meet Edward to try to persuade him not to fight, but the English king felt the urge of his noblemen to engage.

In preparation, a cavalry unit was sent to reconnoitre the Scottish position and its leader Humphrey Bohun came face to face with Robert the Bruce at the summit of a hill. As Bohun charged with a lance, Bruce dispatched his assailant with a single blow from his axe. The encounter seemed to prefigure the larger

outcome, as the English never really recovered from this demoralising setback. The following morning, in an impetuous effort, the cavalry charged uphill at a phalanx of Scotsmen set with pikes that sunk sickeningly into the oncoming horses. A fierce hand-to-hand battle followed and witless English archers stationed behind them started shooting arrows into the backs of their own men.

Amid the confusion, there suddenly appeared over the hill a swarm of marauding Scottish irregulars. The English fled in disarray and hundreds were cut down trying to escape across the marsh. Edward rode up to the castle. Mowbray refused him, forcing the king to flee eastwards and board a waiting ship. Meanwhile some 1600 Englishmen were captured.

Despite being outnumbered three to one, the Scots won a famous victory in a single day. The battle proved decisive as Edward's army was forced to exit Scotland for good. Thus Bannockburn lives on in Scottish memories as the day when the old enemy was finally vanquished. No English king has subsequently ever conquered Scotland.

Pansy Meets Grisly End
Not all is proper in the reign of Edward II

Across the entire span of the Middle Ages just three kings were deposed by violence off the battlefield: Edward II, Richard II and Henry VI. All three had something in common which accounted for their fate. Each had a liking for incompetent favourites who engendered hatred among the nobles and people alike.

No sooner had Edward II been sworn in as king than he introduced to the court a 'friend', an effeminate French knight, Piers de Gaveston, with whom the new king appeared to be infatuated. Not only was this

'upstart' granted more power than any other advisor in the king's company, but, confident in his royal favour, he would cavort about upsetting and humiliating other nobles around him.

Gaveston would greet them not in the usual courteous manner expected in gracious circles but with nicknames: the earl of Warwick became the 'Black Hound of Arden'; the earl of Lancaster, 'Churl'; the earl of Lincoln, 'Burstbelly'; and the earl of Gloucester, 'Horeson'. Before long Edward was obliged to banish the troublesome knave, but within a year had reinstated him. Trouble bestirred.

Edward himself went through the proper motions of marrying, indeed the beautiful princess Isabella, daughter of King Philip IV of France, and together they had children. But this union was severely undermined by his homosexual relationship with Gaveston. The queen eventually joined ranks with Edward's resentful barons and challenged his authority. The result was civil war.

A league of nobles forced the king to agree to a council of 'Ordainers' charged with running the country in his place. Top of the agenda was the banishment of Gaveston. Again, he complied, yet soon returned. Forced into an act of deceit, the Ordainers pretended to offer him safe passage to France if he surrendered. Accepting their terms, Gaveston was instead led to Scarborough Castle where he fell into the hands – certainly not the arms – of his worst enemy, the earl of Warwick, or 'Black Hound of Arden'. This time there would be no escape. Gaveston was summarily executed.

Exasperated nation

This liaison apart, Edward failed in other important duties as defender of the realm. He lost all the territory of Scotland his father had so determinedly won. In fact the Scots even made incursions into the north of England, reaching as far as York.

If this did not end his credibility as king, Edward's next move surely did. Seemingly with no care for the consequences, he introduced to the court a new French lover in the shape of Hugh le Despenser and showered him with all the extravagant favours enjoyed by his predecessor. Enough was enough. Queen Isabella now amassed an army under joint

leadership with her lover Richard Mortimer, and with some ease overran the country. Edward was captured and imprisoned in Berkeley Castle in Gloucestershire. The end was nigh.

Locked in a secure bedchamber, the king was subjected to a series of horrific tortures. It was said that the device used was subtle enough as to leave no mark on the royal body. While cushions were held over Edward's head, a plumber's heated soldering iron was thrust into his bowels. One wag of the time confided, 'He who lives up the arse, dies up it.'

The regicide officially remained a mystery, and Edward's many enemies had got satisfaction. However, Isabella and Mortimer would not survive their triumph long either. The heir to the throne, Edward III, avenged his father's murder by having Mortimer executed and consigning his mother to a nunnery for the rest of her days.

Order of the Garter is Toast of the Town

Edward III leads a golden age of chivalry

In a century that witnessed deep discord between king and country, Edward II's accession to the throne came as a welcome relief. Here at last was a monarch his subjects could respect. He gave to a society which prided itself on chivalry the opportunity to prove itself.

The pomp and pageantry of knightly service flourished as never before under Edward. Setting out to recreate the glamorous world of Arthur and his noble knights at

Camelot, Edward founded a new order in chivalry known as the Order of the Garter after his great victory at the Battle of Crécy in 1348.

At a Round Table tournament held in Windsor to honour his magnificent fighting corps, there was a moment when Edward graciously stooped to pick up the slipped garter of the Countess of Salisbury. As he did so, the king reprimanded his mocking courtiers with the words, '*Honi soit qui mal y pense*' – 'Evil to him who evil thinks'. The utterance was adopted as the proud motto of the Order, which became the highest honour in the land and is still awarded in the Garter Chapel at Windsor Castle.

Ironically, 1348 was the year when much of the nation was reduced to its knees, not in chivalrous gesture but in abject misery, as the Black Death plague swept in from the continent wiping out a third of the population. The fall out was such that even seven years later the king was complaining of plague detritus on the River Thames blocking the passage of the royal barge.

However, for three decades Edward led by example, pursuing his ambition to be king of France. Lords and squires delighted in the chance to prove their courage and to make a fortune from ransoms obtained from prisoners-of-war. Extravagance, ostentatiousness and vanity were all qualities the king possessed – and all were admired by his people.

THE LONGBOW REVOLUTION

Famous English victories over the French at Crécy, Poitiers and Agincourt can all be attributed to a new development in warfare: the longbow. Its range was accurate up to 250 metres and could be shot more rapidly than the conventional crossbow. As one French chronicler recorded, the longbowmen 'shot their arrows with such force and quickness that it seemed as if it snowed'. The longbow also brought about the decline of feudal chivalry as knights on horseback, previously dominant in the battlefield, were helpless against its arrows, which pierced chainmail armour. As the French discovered, to attack skilled archers was to court disaster.

Child King Survives a Nest of Vipers
How Richard II found his character

Richard II was a child for the first eight years of his reign. Unlike his strong father, who had gained the romantic soubriquet of Black Prince for his dashing exploits on the battle field dressed in menacing black armour, Richard was a physical weakling, a callow youth invested with a heavy responsibility he felt he could hardly bear.

Having little appetite for royal duty, Richard chafed at the restrictions imposed by his office. Yet he was brought up to believe he must fulfil the divinity which 'doth hedge in a king'. This conflict in Richard's character found its resolution in the most challenging moment of his royal life: the Peasant's Revolt.

Trouble began in his realm in 1380 when his government tried to impose a new poll tax (on every head of the population). The poor would bear the burden the most. When tax collectors were sent out the following spring to haul in the dues, they were met with fierce resistance and this sparked a widespread revolt.

Gangs of peasants in Essex and Kent ransacked manor houses and burned down property. Whole towns would fall into the hands of the rebels. The Church was a target too, seen to be too wealthy, its tithe too punitive – even the archbishop's palace in Canterbury was burnt to the ground. The army of countryfolk then marched on London and found little resistance; indeed many citizens were sympathetic to their cause.

Facing the music

The peasants, however, claimed they had not risen against the king, but his corrupt ministers. Richard watched anxiously from the battlements of the Tower of London as flames leapt into the sky from one baronial residence after another.

As the situation reached melting point, the nervous 14 year-old king announced, much to everyone's surprise, that he would meet the rebels. On June 15, in an escort of some 200 courtiers and soldiers, Richard rode out to Smithfield, a large open space outside the City walls, which even then served as a cattle market. Drawn up in massed ranks, the angry hordes must have been highly intimidating to such a small detachment. In the boldest voice he could muster, Richard summoned their leader to come

forward. A redundant soldier with a loud mouth, Wat Tyler, had assumed leadership among the rebels and presented himself.

He demanded the abolition of serfdom: 'Let no man be the lord of another,' he bellowed, 'but all should be equal under the king.' He then became abusive and one among the royal retinue recognised Tyler and shouted out that he was the 'greatest thief in all Kent'. Drawing his sword, Tyler tried to advance to the king but was barred by the Lord Mayor, William Walworth. In the following scuffle, Tyler was stabbed in the shoulder and run through.

As the leader fell to the ground dead, the royal party may have thought thier number was up. Then, just as the peasants were drawing their bows, Richard suddenly rode towards them with hand held high.

'Sirs,' he shouted, 'will you shoot your king? I will be your chief and captain and you shall have from me all that you ask.' The king had crucially managed to buy some time and rode with the rebels to Clerkenwell, while his soldiers returned to the palace to drum up support.

Royal vindication

For one long hour Richard negotiated with the rough insurgents. At last he saw the mayor's forces arrive and slowly encircle the rebels. Summoning his royal authority as best he could, Richard called a halt to the meeting and with immense relief saw what had been an implacable enemy slowly disperse. The situation was defused, and before long the uprising was crushed. Richard's proud boast at the end of that day of reckoning was really the young king's supreme rite of passage: 'Let us rejoice and praise God,' he proclaimed, 'for I have this day recovered my lost heritage.'

Murky Rise of House of Lancaster
Henry Bolingbroke plots downfall of Richard II

Henry Bolingbroke's rise to the top was a chequered affair. His father was the powerful John of Gaunt (third son of Edward III) who had guided his errant nephew Richard II through stormy waters early in his reign. When Henry – only a few months older than Richard

– was appointed one of five 'Lords Appellant', or counsellors, to rule over the king, he had to suffer a prolonged enmity from this royal cousin, especially when the king came of age and ruled in his own right.

On one occasion when Henry had a spat with one of his dukes, King Richard decided their quarrel should be settled by a gentleman's duel. An elaborate pageant was organised. Then, just as the contenders were about to engage, Richard waved the whole thing off, sending both into exile, Henry for ten years.

Salt was further rubbed into the wound when, on the death of Henry's father in February of 1399, Richard commuted this ten-year sentence to life and promptly confiscated all his inheritance in the duchy of Lancaster. The landless, exiled duke could only plot his revenge – which he did with ruthless determination.

Gaining the upper hand

The right moment to make his move came a few months later when Richard was away in Ireland sorting out the conflict of rule. His enemy landed at Ravenspur in Yorkshire,

claiming he merely wished to retrieve his rightful inheritance. Though initially having a force of only 300 men, Henry quickly gathered more support in the north as one discontented baron after another joined him, including one Henry Percy, earl of Northumberland.

The king, knowing his position in the realm to be vulnerable, was anxious to return but was delayed by storms. When he did finally land at Conwy Castle in July, he discovered his support had ebbed away. Tricked into believing he could remain as king if he accepted terms offered by Percy, now in the pay of Henry Bolingbroke, he was captured as he left the castle and thrown in prison.

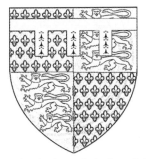

Arms of Richard II with the fleurs-de-lys of France and lions of England

The next item of royal news came in September, namely that Richard II had abdicated in the face of 33 charges brought against him by parliament. Having 'legitimately' disposed of Richard's right to rule, Henry Bolingbroke claimed the throne 'by right line of blood', and more persuasively because the country was in chaos.

The following February brought further news of the abdicated king, this time of his death while in custody at Pontefract Castle. Rumours were rife as to the manner of his demise. Some say he died violently, others that he was slowly starved to death.

Whichever way, it amounted to murder and was committed under orders from his bitter enemy, Henry IV. Thus began the rule of the House of Lancaster, and with it the bitter struggle for power against the rival House of York, who of course always maintained its crown was usurped. The struggle would culminate in the Wars of the Roses half a century later.

French Crown Slips from Henry V's Grasp
Hard graft ends in twist of fate

There were two iconic kings that Henry VIII wished to emulate: Arthur and Henry V. The latter, an ambitious Lancastrian whose military genius made him a legend in his own lifetime, came to within an ace of achieving what had eluded all his ancestors: winning the French throne for England.

It was the Battle of Agincourt, of course, that has gone down in English history as the great landmark in patriotic aspiration. The spirit of Agincourt is invoked whenever morale needs lifting up, and especially when our backs are to the wall. Shakespeare has immortalised the event with his stirring words put into the mouth of Henry V:

Once more unto the breach, dear friends, once more;
Or close the wall up with our English dead.

And so it was, on October 25, 1415, some 20 miles inland of

Boulogne, that this warrior king urged on his 6,000 foot soldiers in the face of a French army numbering in excess of 20,000 – some accounts say as many as 50,000 – including the flower of their cavalry. One might question the king's wisdom in subjecting so many of his 'dear friends' – husbands and fathers among them – to what must have appeared to be an early bloodbath, had it not been for one weapon: the longbow, the fear of the French.

Indeed, Henry himself was by all accounts surprised at the ease of his progress. On landing in Normandy he was expecting a quick raid. Instead the apparent disarray of the French allowed him a fantastic victory against all odds, through clever tactics, clever use of his prize weapon, and 'clever' rain that bogged down the enemy cavalry.

AGE OF ARMOUR

By the beginning of the 15th century, old-fashioned chain mail had been replaced by plate armour. This protective wear was difficult to forge; great centres existed at Milan, in Italy; Augsburg and Nuremburg in Germany. But at Agincourt, even the new armour was found to be vulnerable to the deadly power and accuracy of the longbow. Armour continued to be worn in battle until guns and gunpowder finally made it redundant in the 16th century.

Quickening the chase

The French lost 7,000 men, among them the finest of their nobility. Their country was left defenceless and leaderless in the face of England's determined 28 year-old king. By contrast the English had lost less than 100, and only one lord.

Pressing home his advantage, Henry continued the onslaught for another four years, capitalising on a France divided by civil war between the great families of Armagnac and Burgundy. Finally, in 1419, the influential duke of Burgundy capitulated and recognised Henry as unofficial king of France. Within months the whole country was under English control.

The following year Henry married Catherine, daughter of Charles VI of France, on the understanding he was heir to the French throne. The old king was ailing. It was surely only a matter of time before Henry could lay his hands on the crown. Alas a bout dysentery was to cruelly deny him – and just a month later the French king followed Henry to the grave. His baby son would succeed him, as Henry VI, but lose all that his illustrious father had gained.

Architect of Eton Not Interested in Ruling
Henry VI more monk than king

Henry was just eight months old when he inherited the crown on the death of his father, Henry V, in 1422. His uncles governed as regents for the next 15 years. He had to wait until he was old enough to be able to support a crown before he could undergo such a demanding ceremony as the coronation.

This he did when eight. Even then, the crown was too heavy for the boy to wear unaided, so it was held aloft while litanies were sung. To ease the burden of such an ordeal, a sumptuous feast was laid on with all the young royal's favourites, including 'roast meat fritters' and jelly. Little

did Henry know that a few hundred miles south a young French maid, nine years his senior, would in the same year lead an army of 4000 soldiers to champion the rights of French freedom from the English yoke. He might also not have been aware that the following year this girl, Joan of Arc, was burnt at the stake on the ground of being a witch. The French surely lost just the sort of mascot they needed to unite them.

Just nine months later Henry, now eleven, took part in a second elaborate coronation, this time in Paris, to crown him king of France.

Henry VI was the only sovereign to be crowned in both England and Wales

The prize for which his father devoted so much of his hard-fought life to win came effortlessly to his son. Perhaps it is not surprising that Henry VI lacked interest in keeping a grip on the French throne, for he had been handed it on a plate at a tender age. When the tide turned against the English and their crucial alliance with Burgundy broke down, Henry is said to have burst into tears.

While the kingdom of France gradually slipped from English hands, the finer sensibilities of Henry's character fed a different sort of ambition, in the direction of architecture, learning and Christian piety. Meanwhile his mother Catherine, widow to Henry V, formed a new liaison with a Welshman, Owen Tudor, a union destined to have a lasting impact on the English throne.

Gothic wonders

In the 50 years of what turned out to be a disastrous reign, Henry VI left behind one tangible legacy: the buildings that express his own qualities of faith and devotion to learning. The chapels he commissioned at King's College

Cambridge and at Eton are considered to reach a high point in the Gothic style that dominated European architecture for four centuries. One hundred metres of soaring columns and delicate fan vaulting in the Chapel of King's College lead the eye to a mesmerizing stained glass window above the high altar.

Henry's idea in founding Eton in 1440 was to provide free instruction 'in the rudiments of grammar' to anyone except 'bastards' and 'the unfree', as a preparation for higher learning at King's College Cambridge.

Yorkist Star Rises
Edward IV flies in the face of 'Kingmaker'

For 30 years in the 15th century England was torn by the vicious struggle between rival pretenders to the throne. The source of the conflict lay in the deep bitterness of dynastic rivalry. From the sons of Edward III had sprung two great families, the houses of York and Lancaster, each believing it had the legitimate claim to the throne.

Open conflict did not break out until the 1450s when the Hundred Years War with France came to an end. Military minds could then focus on the reign of Lancaster's Henry VI, whose weakness and increasing insanity seemed to invite an opportunist to grab the reins. Into this apparent power vacuum strode the impressive Edward IV, tall handsome and warrior-like – quite unlike his Lancastrian counterpart.

Grey lady

The woman Edward chose to be his wife, Elizabeth Woodville, was young and beautiful, but of low birth and, more important, Lancastrian. Edward kept the marriage under wraps. When at last he was asked in public whom he should marry, after a moment of embarrassment he confessed his secret. His wife was also a widow; her married name being Grey, of the same family that would produce the hapless Lady Jane of the next century.

Kingmaker

The intrigues of the ensuing Wars of the Roses are too complex to cover here but it is curious that such a

militaristic name for three decades of conflict involved scarcely half a dozen battles. The clashes tended to go over the heads of the ordinary people – taking place as they did in the palaces of the south and dour castles of the north. In that sense the conflict didn't constitute a civil war either.

Despite Edward's military prowess and popularity, he did not bargain for the power of the 'Kingmaker', as Richard Neville, earl of Warwick, came to be known. Owner of vast wealth across the Midlands his will, more than any other's, carried the day.

When half way through the long struggle Warwick switched allegiance to the exiled Henry, King Edward was forced to flee, coming close to drowning in The Wash as he dashed across the North Sea for refuge. Thereupon, the now mad Henry was reinstated on the throne, albeit briefly.

When Edward returned a year later, in 1471, to avenge himself, the Yorkist king was triumphant on the battlefields of Barnet and Tewkesbury. The Lancastrian armies were shattered and, as important, the earl of Warwick was dead. The way was clear for Edward to resume his kingship.

Henry was dispatched to the Tower where he lost his head, literally, and Edward ruled for another 12 years, quite a feat in wartime.

THE PRINTING PRESS

England's first ever printed book was made in Edward IV's reign. The book, entitled **Dictes and Sayenges of the Phylosophers,** *may not have made for easy bedtime reading but it did allow a proud moment for its maker William Caxton when he presented it on bended knee to the king. Using revolutionary technology from Germany, this wealthy wool merchant set up the first printing press in England. Previously, manuscripts had to be laboriously copied longhand. Now they could be reproduced in their hundreds, and they included the first printed copy of Chaucer's* **Canterbury Tales.**

Wicked Uncle or Cornered Rat?
Did Richard III really deserve his evil image?

Too often Richard III's career is judged by his murder of the Princes in the Tower. The bad press that blackened his character came from two main sources, both posthumous: the biased biographer of Henry VII, who defeated Richard III on the field of Bosworth, and William Shakespeare, who may have read this biography for his information and from it created the caricature of the king we see as a monstrous hunchback.

It is on record that the two Princes were held in the Tower, never to be seen again, and that Richard was responsible for their deaths. Even by 15th century standards the double murder of two innocent children was horrific, and no doubt contributed to Richard's downfall.

But many wonder if history has yet judged him unfairly. For 30 of the 33 years of his life, Richard was a conscientious administrator and general, deeply loyal to his brother

Edward IV, and a faithful husband. Indeed, were he to have died in 1483 instead of his brother, he would have gone down in history as a decent chap. So why did everything go horribly wrong?

Background intrigue

The political intrigues that constantly fuelled the Wars of the Roses came to a precipitate conclusion in the events that led to that decisive Battle of Bosworth. The nub of the matter, as always, was to do with dynastic succession. Once the

ruling monarch – in this case Edward IV – was dead rival claimants would scurry for supremacy.

Now, Edward IV's queen, Elizabeth Woodville, was set on promoting her son and heir apparent, Edward, to be the next king. But this was complicated by the fact that his uncle Richard, who had so ably supported Edward IV in his affairs of state had been nominated in his will as Protector of the young prince. At this stage, did Richard have designs on the throne or was he content to usher his nephew to it?

Once Edward IV was dead, Elizabeth, being born of lowly stock, was nervous of her position and feared that Richard might gather the aristocracy to support his bid for the crown. Furthermore, many nobles, perhaps including Richard, blamed the queen and her advisors for the death of Richard's other brother Clarence, who had been sentenced to death for treason. Richard was said to be 'overcome with grief', and duly set up two religious foundations to pray for his dead brother and other members of the royal family. A court chronicler of the time wrote that the Woodvilles 'were afraid that if Richard took the crown, they who bore the blame of Clarence's death would suffer death or at least be ejected from their high estate'.

Dog eat dog

Therefore, after her royal husband's death in April 1483, the queen arranged for her son Edward to be brought from Ludlow to London as quickly as possible for safety sake. The trouble was, too many lords of the land supported Richard in preference to the queen, and through them Richard got wind of her plans. At this point it has to be asked, what was his best course of action?

Queen Elizabeth's intentions were clear. She was going to get her young son crowned as soon as possible. Indeed preparations were being made for a coronation on 24 June, just weeks away. Once Richard's responsibility as Protector was dissolved, he would be vulnerable. For Edward, aged twelve, was considered in those days to be nearly an adult. On becoming king, he was not going to favour Richard over his own mother. The solution was simple: to survive, Richard had to rule,

and to rule he had to be king. It was a dog-eat-dog situation.

Kidnap

So, on hearing the news that the young prince was travelling to London, Richard and his men headed south, kidnapped the prince and took him to the Tower. The rest, as they say, is history. Richard had also to kidnap the second of Elizabeth's sons to eliminate his possible accession.

A rumour was circulated that the princes were bastards in any case. With power to his elbow, Richard had little difficulty in persuading parliament to present him with the crown in the absence of legitimate contenders.

Though he won this round, Richard was still up against it. For Elizabeth would not lie down easily. Though she had given up hope of ever seeing her two sons again, she could wrest the crown from this Yorkist usurper by presenting one Henry Tudor, sole surviving Lancastrian claimant, with the hand of her daughter in marriage. She being the daughter of Edward IV would help Tudor's cause to rule. And so it was, when Richard fell on the field at Bosworth in 1485 – the last English king to die in battle – that the Plantagenet dynasty came to an end, to be replaced by the Tudors. It was a milestone in English history. From now on, the country was no longer beset by medieval struggles in arms but bloomed in the growing prosperity of the modern era.

Patron of Expansion
Henry VII commissions Cabot to set sail

Under the guidance of Henry VII the country laid the foundation of future Tudor strength. Efficient and continuous government, without the enervating preoccupation with war that beset every Plantagenet administration, enabled the nation's energies to create wealth. The wool and cloth industries expanded bringing more sterling than ever before into the nation's coffers.

Henry VII was probably the first businessman to be king of England. Not only did he quietly set about building up the country, he was astute enough to seize an opportunity when it came his way.

That opportunity came in the form of an Italian navigator named John Cabot. Having pondered the news of Columbus's discovery of America five years earlier, Henry had thought of commissioning the Spanish explorer to search out new sources of wealth overseas for British commercial interests. When Cabot turned up with his own promises to find new ocean routes to Japan and China – which were thought to be accessible by sailing west across the Atlantic – Henry was delighted to fund him.

The king made available all that Bristol had to offer, with its long

heritage in shipping. Accompanied by 20 English mariners, Cabot set sail from Bristol quay aboard the *Matthew* in 1497 and crossed the Atlantic in 35 days – the first seafarer to cross the northern Atlantic since the Vikings. Unsure of where he had made landfall, Cabot simply named the place New-Found Land, and planted the Tudor flag and standard of St Mark, the symbol of Venice.

Returning to England amid much confusion about where or what he had discovered, most agreed it must be northern Asia, and that the highly valued spice islands would be but a short sail away. The king rewarded the captain's daring deed with the sum of £10, plus a pension of £20 a year, and, perhaps of greater importance, the promise of a second venture, this time with a larger fleet.

Alas the voyage got lost among the icebergs of Greenland and was forced home. Not long afterwards, Henry VII breathed his last. But the expeditions had set the tone for a century of exploration that would turn the realm into an empire.

RED BRICK REVOLUTION

Although we associate Tudor red brick mansions with the like of Hampton Court, built in Henry VIII's reign, the craze for this new style of architecture began in the reign of Henry VII. In 1500 he commissioned the extravagant Richmond Palace (named after his previous title), built in the manner of the grand houses of Flanders and Burgundy, with fancy turrets and long bay windows. The revolution spread quickly through the country as wealthy wool and cloth merchants built themselves fortified manor houses in the characteristic brick and timber-frame style, designed more for decoration and banquets than defence.

Canny Scot Eyes Opportunity

James IV considers alliance with 'Richard IV' of England

Never happy with the border line that separated England from their country, the Scots took certain opportunities when they arose to raid the northern counties of England.

One highly respected king, who was reputedly obsessed with the arts of war, was 23 year-old James IV, who made several such raids successfully in the 1490s.

In a bid to expand his military ambition, James entertained the idea of allying himself to a pretender to the English throne in the person of Perkin Warbeck. The 22 year-old Warbeck claimed to be none other than Edward IV's son, Richard duke of York, whom everyone in England believed had perished in the Tower at the hands of his enemy Richard III.

Living in exile, Purbeck further claimed to have support from the Holy Roman Emperor Maximilian. Having tried to land at Deal in Kent in 1495 and been defeated by Henry VII's defences, Warbeck was welcomed by James at his court in Edinburgh. Indeed the Englishman was accepted as Richard IV and even married off to the king's cousin.

SYPHILIS

Unwelcome to the Scottish court were Warbeck's soldiers who brought with them the earliest known instances of syphilis in the British Isles. The disease is thought to have emanated from the New World and been brought to Europe by Columbus's sailors who then enlisted in the siege of Naples. Among Warbeck's men were mercenaries who had been at Naples. James IV ordered all carriers to assemble for treatment, which involved the application of mercury, believed to be a cure.

Much to Warbeck's disappointment, however, James was not prepared to undertake a serious challenge to Henry VII's forces, with or without his ally's support. Instead, the Scottish king decided on a truce, one which ushered in a new era of peace after two centuries of intermittent conflict.

In 1503, by way of confirmation of this treaty, James married Margaret Tudor, daughter of Henry VII, at Holyrood Palace in Edinburgh. The Stewart thistle and Tudor rose became symbolically entwined in political union. With the death of Henry VII's eldest son Arthur the previous year, Margaret was now second in line to the throne. Should anything happen to the English king's second son, Henry, the English throne would pass to James Stewart.

However, a leopard never changes its spots. James could not resist the opportunity to have one more go at the old enemy when Louis XII of France waged war with England, leaving the north country open to attack. Alas, the Scot underestimated the strength of the English army and came unstuck. At the Battle of Flodden he and 10,000 of his countrymen lost their lives in one of the biggest slaughters ever by the English foe.

FIRST SCOTCH WHISKY

The earliest reference to Scotch whisky comes from an entry in the Scottish Exchequer Rolls in 1495. Friar John Cor was granted malt with which to distil about 1500 bottles for the court of James IV, who was known to be fond of the drink. Until then Scotch had been monopolised by surgeon-barbers who used it for medicinal purposes when treating diseases.

Visionary Supremo
Why did Henry VIII not abandon his Supremacy once he had a son as heir?

Probably the most famous thing about Henry VIII is his six wives. We know that he had one after another principally to bear a son and heir to his Tudor throne, that he was even prepared to break with the Pope and form a whole new Church in order to see through this desire.

So the question arises, when his third wife Jane Seymour successfully

delivered a healthy son, who would in time become Edward VI, why did Henry not make life easier for himself and abandon his policy of Royal Supremacy over the pope and return England to the Roman Catholic fold? The job was done, future of the Tudor dynasty secured.

Henry had engendered huge opposition within the Church, not least by dissolving the monasteries, a policy that provoked outrage everywhere and prompted the worst crisis of his reign, the Pilgrimage of Grace rebellion of 1536.

PILGRIMAGE OF GRACE
When the king began his policy of monastic 'reform' that resulted in mass closure he cannot have expected the scale of the reaction from the clergy, whom he thought could easily be bought off with a pension. But for the monks the dissolution brought home just what the break with Rome meant. By the end, more than 800 monasteries and abbeys were destroyed or closed down.
A full-scale revolt started, led by monks and abbots. Their ranks quickly swelled to 30,000 as they

took control of the north and marched south to Doncaster to meet Henry's tiny army, by comparison, of 8000. The king faced the biggest challenge of his reign.

However, the monks were persuaded that their quarrel was not really with the king but with his advisors, especially chancellor Thomas Cromwell. When promised a pardon, most dispersed, probably not having the stomach for a fight anyway. The ringleaders, though, were arrested and some suffered dreadfully in the Tower for their pains.

The answer to why Henry did not abandon his Act of Supremacy can be seen in a contemporary painting by Hans Holbein, depicting the Tudor dynasty. Henry VIII stands with his wife Jane Seymour either side of a monument telling of the greatnesses of the Tudor kings. Behind it stands his father Henry VII and mother Elizabeth of York. On the face of the stone is inscribed verses in Latin, which translated ask the question: 'Which is greater, the father or son?' The answer given is that Henry Tudor 'was great for ending the Wars of the

Roses, but Henry VIII was greater, indeed the greatest, for while he was King true religion was restored and the power of Popes trodden underfoot.'

Although Henry had broken with Rome in the first place simply to gain a divorce from Catherine of Aragon, the king had become proud of his achievement in establishing his own Church, one which would stand for all time in memorial to him. Henry had done what no monarch before him had ever managed, though countless times they might have wished to be independent of the power wielded at Rome.

Just to ram home the point, a new English translation of the Bible displayed on its title page a representation of an elevated throne surrounded by ecclesiastic and lay figures. Seated on the throne is not Christ, who is a tiny figure hovering above, but a rather corpulent Henry VIII regally dispensing scripture.

What Henry did not foresee was that his creation would take on a life of its own, guided by others, with whom he and his successors might not necessarily agree. In so doing he

had given birth to Protestantism, and a form of it that would ultimately destroy the monarchy in the next century.

King with Socialist Agenda
Edward VI points the way to care of the underprivileged

W hen Jane Seymour bore a son and heir to the Tudor throne in 1537, after an emergency Caesarean section, Bishop Latimer said, 'We all hungered after a prince so long that there was as much rejoicing as at the birth of John the Baptist.' The treasured prince was naturally given every possible care and attention throughout his upbringing.

Edward turned out to be a precocious boy who enjoyed debates with his tutors and advisors. His education took a humanist tendency and this manifested itself later in his short reign as king after the death of Henry VIII in 1547. He was perhaps the first royal socialist reformer.

England lagged behind other countries of Europe in education. Some two-thirds of the populace remained illiterate. In an attempt to alleviate the plight of the poor, Edward created various institutions.

He turned over to the City the unwanted Bridewell Palace, built at great expense by his father, for it to be converted into a workhouse for the destitute. It would also house the homeless and serve as a place of correction for prostitutes and idlers.

Edward founded a school in London, called Christ's Hospital, for the growing number of orphans found on the streets. He is perhaps better known for creating a string of grammar schools up and down the country. And he requisitioned various chantries (chapels for the singing of mass), which he considered would be put to better use if they served educational purposes.

Premises for the Commons

In the Palace of Westminster, Edward set aside one chapel for a special purpose. St Stephen's would be converted into a permanent office for the parliamentary Commons to sit in.

Until now, the Commons had no fixed abode and would have to make do with any space that might be vacant at the time, sometimes it was just a refectory.

The layout of the former chapel accounts for much of today's structure and workings of the House of Commons. The Speaker's chair was positioned where the altar used to be, and may account for why MPs bow to the Speaker when addressing him or her. Members sat in the choir stalls, conveniently facing each other in adversarial style. And at each end · of the choir screen were doors to the vestry – these now form part of the voting system: through the one to the right pass the 'aye' voters, to the left the 'no' voters.

Most of the chapel was destroyed in the fire of 1834. Struck down by tuberculosis at the age of 15, Edward was one of the few kings of England to date who acted on a social conscience.

Lady Jane Grey Faints on Hearing News
England's nine-day queen

Had Edward VI not developed tuberculosis, Lady Jane Grey might have lived a lot longer than she did. She might well have married him, her second cousin, for the two were close companions at the royal court and almost the same age. Instead this great-granddaughter of Henry VII and daughter of Henry Grey, duke of Suffolk, was cruelly manipulated at the age of 15 by the duke of Northumberland, regent and power behind the throne. He persuaded the dying Edward to bequeath his crown to the devout Protestant Jane instead of his elder sister Mary, who, it was feared, would turn the country back to Rome.

Extraordinary 'Device'

But what was going through Edward's mind when he signed this will? By leaving the throne to Lady Jane he was clearly transgressing the Act of Succession which his father Henry VIII had laid down as inviolable law. In this settlement all three of his children – Edward, Mary and Elizabeth – were named as potential heirs. Edward and Northumberland's ploy – based on the pretext that both Mary and Elizabeth had been bastardised and were therefore illegitimate – was at once illegal and placed the Crown above Parliament and the law. Even Lady Jane's most ardent Protestant supporters might have baulked at that. But the sickly 15 year-old king believed that he possessed divine authority which allowed him to vary his father's edict. So he drafted his 'Device for the succession'.

Perhaps the plotters' greatest mistake was not to arrest Mary, the legitimate heir, at once. Without a doubt, while still free she was not going to accept Lady Jane's enthronement in her place, and might be able to rouse sufficient support for her cause in the country.

Two queens proclaimed

Northumberland's conspirators at first kept secret the king's death on July 6, 1553, while final preparations were made. Even Lady Jane was taken aback when eventually they proclaimed her to be the new Queen of England on July 10. At first she refused, saying Mary was rightful heir. When her counsellors informed her she was Edward's chosen successor, she is said to have fainted on the spot. But persuaded that this was no less than God's will, Jane eventually consented.

For her security the reluctant Queen was rowed from Syon House to the Tower of London. Alas, this would be her first – and last – state journey.

Meanwhile Mary, having fled London, entrenched herself at Framlingham Castle in Suffolk and proclaimed herself to be rightful queen. The next few days proved critical. It soon became apparent to Northumberland that Mary was gaining much more support than he anticipated. As he rode north with an army to force her submission, he wrote, 'The people press to see us, but no one sayeth God speed us.'

Once the movement had begun to roll in favour of Mary, it quickly gathered momentum. Within days of Northumberland's departure, the plot had fallen apart.

Father arrests daughter

Back in London the Privy Council changed their allegiance and backed Mary. Even Lady Jane's father had to turn against his own daughter and sadly arrested her on July 19.

After the collapse of Northumberland's campaign, Mary as new queen found it in herself to reverse Lady Jane's death sentence on compassionate grounds. She was allowed to live with her husband, Lord Dudley, son of the duke of Northumberland, under house arrest in the Tower.

By the following January, however, circumstances had changed and the Queen felt sufficiently threatened by rebellion to renew the verdict. Even then, Jane was offered a reprieve if she recanted on her Protestant faith, but her conscience would not permit it, and instead she opted graciously for the executioner's block.

Phantom Pregnancy Changes All
Mary I's popularity turns sour without heir

When Londoners greeted Mary I's victory over the usurper Lady Jane Grey, their unbounded joy left the new Queen dazed with wonder. An eyewitness wrote, 'I never saw the like. The bonfires were without number, and what with the shouting and crying of the people, and ringing of bells, there could no one man hear what another said.'

The uproarous triumph that accompanied Mary's accession was mostly to do with seeing the monarchy put back on the right track with orderly succession that would find God's favour and therefore national well being. All depended on right dynastic succession. In turn, Mary's limelight would remain bright only if she, now 37, could deliver an heir.

Pressure builds
Mary's marriage to the Catholic Philip II of Spain did cause some anxiety. Indeed spontaneous rebellions demonstrated there was a good deal of antipathy towards the return of the national faith to Roman Catholicism and the Pope.

But when the Queen announced she was pregnant in April 1555, many of the concerns melted away. With an heir to the throne in the offing, Mary and Philip were able to persuade Parliament to overturn Henry VIII's Act of Royal Supremacy and obey the Pope. Then they set about eliminating Protestant opposition. The burnings began.

Over the course of three years, more than 300 men and women became martyrs for their faith. Many

more scuttled into exile rather than face the stake.

Change of wind

Then the tide began to turn for Mary. Amid growing excitement at the imminent arrival of a royal son or daughter, it gradually became apparent that there was going to be no child, no heir to the throne. It was a phantom pregnancy.

In an instant Mary's world was turned upside down. She became a laughing stock. People jeered her and spread stories that she had given birth to a monkey. Her husband threw up his hands and left for Spain.

Furthermore a Protestant account of the horrors of the burnings, *Foxe's Book of Martyrs*, was published at the same time and became a best seller. In it the author coined the appellation, 'Bloody Mary', and so it stuck for all time.

Destitute

Abandoned by her husband and with age against her, Mary's prospects of delivering an heir were bleak. As the Protestant revival gathered pace after the heroic martyrdom of archbishop

Cranmer, Mary quietly retreated into her shell and became ill. Even when writing out her will, she still entertained visions of progeny, and stated she wished to pass her crown to her unborn Catholic child. However, when finally on her deathbed, the Queen did amend the wording, to the one who 'by the laws and statutes of this realm' should be her successor. Even at this late stage, the rancour remained and she could not bring herself to mention Elizabeth by name.

Two Cousins Who Never Met
The Scottish and English queens

Mary, Queen of Scots led a colourful life. She was tall with long blond hair, sophisticated, intelligent and though not considered beautiful, it all created a striking image. She had a wild lust for life too. Having inherited the Scottish throne just six days after her birth, the infant Queen was sent to the French court at the age of five, where she was brought up in the grand European manner and learned several languages.

Like most nobles of the time,

Mary thrilled at the chase, enjoying deer hunting when back in Scotland. She played cards and was fond of gambling. Most of all she loved music and would go out dancing in Edinburgh. She even learned to play golf, being one of the first women ever to do so.

This might all seem today to be the natural activities of an exuberant member of the royal family. But in 16th century Scotland it was deeply frowned on. The nation was in the grip of a Calvinist revolution espousing stern principles that did not suffer lightly such frivolities.

In 1560 the Scots outlawed Catholicism, and before long its Catholic queen was fleeing for her life. Rowed across the Solway Firth

in just the clothes she was wearing, Mary sought refuge from her cousin, Elizabeth I of England.

Mary's arrival was treated with caution. As daughter of James V of Scotland and the great-granddaughter of Henry VII, she sat next in line to the English throne, and as such posed a threat to Elizabeth and her Protestant rule. While her counsellors debated what should be done, the two cousins were each curious to know what the other was like.

Elizabeth had long heard tales of her wayward cousin's adventures and in truth was a little jealous of her accomplishments. Already she had got through two husbands and probably a lover. And when it was decided that Mary should be held prisoner indefinitely, the English virgin queen was forever asking questions about her. Whose hair was finer? Which of the two was the more attractive?

Relations slowly soured, however. When the Pope excommunicated Elizabeth in 1580 and called on all Catholics to strive to overthrow the Protestant heretic, Elizabeth became paranoid that Mary was the focus of every conspiracy. Eventually she decided the Scot was too dangerous to live and had her executed. So ended the relationship of the two royal cousins – who never did meet. Until, perhaps, in death when they were buried beside each other in Westminster Abbey.

Faerie Queen from Broken Home
Brave Queen Elizabeth never recovers

A queen with less foreign blood than any previous monarch embodied the patriotic spirit of a nation. The amazing 45 year reign of Elizabeth I transformed a squabbling medieval state on the periphery of Europe into a unified, proud nation capable of defeating the mighty Spanish Armada and exploring the world.

This queen at the helm has gone down in English history as perhaps the most remarkable leader the country has ever known. Yet the glittering success of poet Edmund Spenser's 'Gloriana' belies the dreadful early years of her life – or perhaps they were the making of her life.

Elizabeth came from a broken home. Her father, Henry VIII, had not only divorced her mother, Anne Boleyn, he had her executed and declared Elizabeth to be illegitimate. Unloved, unwanted, her childhood was dominated by tragedy, her fate varying with every alteration in her father's politics.

Her unhappiness continued into adolescence. Under the reign of her brother Edward VI, she came under suspicion after flirting with Thomas Seymour who was executed for treason. Her life took a serious downturn on the succession of her elder sister Mary who became

Elizabeth I was depicted as 'The Faerie Queen' by poet Edmund Spenser

convinced that Elizabeth lay at the heart of a Protestant rebellion.

When taken captive to the Tower of London, she saw en route all the sorry evidence of a failed revolt – heads of executed traitors, for instance, displayed on pikes in the streets. For more than a year she was held in prison, fearing the executioner's visit at any time.

But as she languished there, hope sprang forth. Londoners everywhere secretly sided with Elizabeth. Treasonous notices were scattered in the streets pledging support for her against Mary. A dead cat dressed in a Catholic priest's vestments was strung up on a gallows in Cheapside.

Such signs declared that London was ready to embrace a regime change. A wave of revulsion had spread against its queen, her Spanish husband and their religion. The day Mary I died in 1558 turned Elizabeth's fortunes for good.

Suddenly the new queen could leave behind the baggage of a disturbed childhood and look forward to a time of peace and harmony. But above all, this lonely heart yearned for affection. She soon learned she had a gift for captivating her subjects, including William Shakespeare towards the end of her reign.

Elizabeth made a point of travelling round the country every year to meet her people and lapped up their blessings. Once in Coventry the mayor presented her with a chalice filled with gold. Elizabeth was pleased: 'I have but few such gifts.' The mayor ventured to add, 'If it please your Grace there is a great deal more in it – the hearts of your loving subjects.' 'We thank you', she replied, 'It is a great deal more indeed.'

CULT OF THE FAERIE QUEEN

Elizabeth employed court painters to promote the cult of 'The Faerie Queen', as Edmund Spenser entitled the poem dedicated to her. Its focus was the virgin queen-goddess, Gloriana. As Elizabeth grew older, she is said to have refused to look any more in a mirror, preferring instead to gaze upon the masterpieces of 'faerie' wonder created by her artists who could sustain the belief that her beauty would never fade.

Here was a monarch with an exceptional personality: one of strength, wisdom, courage, yet one that knew its emotional weakness. The wounds of her youth ran deep. Perhaps it is no surprise that Elizabeth courted affection from subjects and suitors alike, that she was inordinately vain and accepted flattery with relish. Yet she would never allow anyone too close. 'It shall be sufficient for me,' she remarked, 'that a marble stone shall declare that a queen, having reigned such a time, lived and died a virgin.'

Eager Scot Opens Can of Worms

James VI of Scotland has no idea what trials await him as James I of England

Of his 59 year life, James was king for 58 of them. And he was King of Scotland for 36 years before even beginning his reign over England, the dual reign lasting another 22 years to 1625.

When James VI of Scotland crossed the border in 1603, it was a momentous occasion. The last time a Scottish monarch had stepped on English soil was almost a century ago. For many Scots the accession to the English throne – by virtue of being great grandson to Henry VIII's sister Margaret – was a conquest in itself. Others were less sure, thinking it may result in the Scots ceding control of their own affairs.

With great excitement, and to much jubilation, James galloped south at tremendous speed, riding in one stretch 40 miles in under four hours, his entourage desperately trying to keep up.

On arriving in London, though the people there also welcomed their new king and new Stuart dynasty, James would find much cause for anxiety.

Unlike his healthy lifestyle north of the border, famine and destitution beset the capital. A massive outbreak of the bubonic plague had struck London in the year of his accession, killing 30,000 inhabitants, one-in-four of its population. On top of that, within a year he narrowly escaped an assassination attempt as the Gunpowder Plot aimed to blow him up at the state opening of Parliament. But perhaps his greatest challenge was fixing a Church riven by dissent.

Puritan trouble

A growing movement of Puritans petitioned the king to make radical reforms to the Church of England in line with their simpler Calvinist worship. They wanted to rid it of elements that smacked of Catholicism: music to be restricted, no bowing, an end to clerical vestments, and many other changes to ritual, which though might seem inconsequential, in sum would radically alter the nature of the Church of England.

Never shy of intellectual debate, James convened a council at Hampton Court to try to settle the matter. He thought the best course to be compromise. But in making concessions to the Puritans, he upset his bishops. In an effort to reassure both camps, James authorized a new translation of the Bible that would be the fruit of both Puritans and Anglican bishops, and therefore bring unity to the Church. Writing in the language of everyday use, 54 scholars laboured for seven years to produce the version that has come down to us as *The King James Bible,* or *Authorized Version.* Unfortunately, despite its enduring value, the 'Good Book'

probably caused more disagreement than harmony. Society was set on the road to civil war.

Flight to New World

Throwing up his arms in despair, the King came to consider the whole Puritan venture to be 'unlawful, and to savour of tumult, sedition and violence'. His fear that it might cause widespread unrest soon prompted him to take a hard line on Puritan dissent. Unless they conformed, James pronounced, he would 'harry them out of the land'. The King's threats were heeded, and in 1608 persecution forced many pilgrims to flee to

Holland in the hope of finding a freer life there.

When this did not materialise, they returned briefly to prepare for what would be the famous migration aboard the *Mayflower*. In 1620 the 'Pilgrim Fathers' set sail across the Atlantic to become the founders of the New World. For two months the ship was home to 101 passengers. Of these, 35 were Puritan 'saints' and another 66 were ordinary folk driven by hardship to seek a better life. What these émigrés did not know, of course, was that within a generation a puritanical Commonwealth, led by Oliver Cromwell, would be constituted in the old country.

INVENTIONS

During his long reign, first of Scotland, then also of England, James witnessed many important innovations. The first water closet was installed at a country home; a microscope was built in the Netherlands to magnify scientific discoveries; a Scottish mathematician discovered logarithms to eliminate tedious calculations. Galileo invented the thermometer and claimed to see mountains on the moon through the new telescope. Hand grenades and a rifle were designed. Even the first submarine appeared: a wooden framed vessel covered in greased leather skin was demonstrated in the Thames.

So Good a Man, So Bad a King
Failed experiment of the principled Charles I

The young Charles I, unlike his father James I, was sober, dignified, handsome and courteous. It was said that he never violated a woman, nor struck a man, nor even spoke an evil word. He lacked his father's intellect but appealed to a generation who valued his integrity.

Charles was a small man; in some paintings he almost disappears into his riding boots. But he had a deep-rooted sense of his own dignity and importance. Set in a delicate frame with a feminine face, his melancholy air almost seemed to mark him out for tragedy.

When Charles unexpectedly

became heir after his elder brother Henry died, his awkwardness and shyness made him rely heavily on trusted advisors. But one of them, the Duke of Buckingham, led Charles disastrously to quarrel with Parliament. In truth, Buckingham probably brought out the King's natural distaste for those beneath him endowed with power.

He decried parliamentarians as having 'the nature of cats', which 'ever grow cursed with age.' Their demands for reform, he believed, would only result in war. So in 1629 he had done with them and abandoned parliamentary government altogether. Charles believed that kings had divine authority to rule. For the next eleven years he pursued a policy known

as 'Thorough', a rule with select ministers for the mutual benefit of all his subjects, in effect a 'benevolent dictatorship'.

This policy worked for a time, but Charles was really only as good as his advisors. Some of them aroused enmity in the country. Thomas Wentworth, earl of Strafford, was nicknamed 'Black Tom the Tyrant' for his brutality in Ireland. When William Laud, archbishop of Canterbury, persuaded Charles to lead an army into Scotland in pursuance of his policy imposing the English Prayer Book on its people, the King came unstuck.

In 1640, he was forced to recall Parliament. The King and his people were now at loggerheads. This time it

Crowds gather outside Banqueting House to witness the first ever public execution of an English king

was civil war. Charles fought for seven years for his throne before his forces suffered a decisive defeat at Naseby in 1645.

Four years later Charles was convicted of treason in Oliver Cromwell's parliament and beheaded outside Banqueting House in Whitehall. To the end Charles I was a man of principle, one who would not sacrifice his beliefs to save his crown.

ENGLAND'S FIRST ARCHITECT

Charles I's declared aim was to create the most civilised court in Europe. He patronised all the leading artists – collecting 1400 paintings himself – and in Inigo Jones the King found the finest architect of his age. Jones transformed English architecture on Classical lines, creating a style whose influence would last 300 years. Among his masterpieces are the Banqueting Hall (on the steps of which Charles was beheaded) in Whitehall, the Queen's House at Greenwich and St Paul's Church, Covent Garden.

Time of Gay Abandon Comes to Woeful End
Charles II liberates devils from Puritan prison

When Charles II came to the throne in 1660 England had suffered nearly two decades of unhappiness. First, a long civil war ended miserably with the execution of her king, then a puritanical Commonwealth ruled the nation, during which all manner of repression prevented the people from enjoying themselves. Virtually every outdoor

recreation had been banned by the Puritans on the ground of being a distraction from the path of God.

Come the Restoration and hunting, wrestling, animal-baiting, tennis, ice-skating and the earliest forms of organized football all reappeared in public. Horse-racing drew large crowds again – principally on the back of Charles's personal patronage of Newmarket race course, where he kept several Arab horses.

The arts flourished again. With

ROYAL OBSERVATORY
Stung by remarks about poor English navigation at a reception for a French visitor, Charles II boasted that his astronomers could chart the movement of the stars with great accuracy. When told that England's equipment was not up to the task, the King ordered Christopher Wren to build an observatory that would outdo all rivals. Thus was produced the Royal Observatory near the Palace of Greenwich. From its Octagonal Room, 'Greenwich Mean Time' was established as the world's temporal yardstick.

the King's encouragement theatres reopened to riotous abandon. New bawdy plays, subsequently known as Restoration Drama, were staged in which actresses were used for the first time, replacing boys who previously acted female roles. One of the first to hit the stage was Nell Gwynne, formerly an orange seller, who so delighted the King she became one of his many mistresses. Charles had set the tone for a lewd society on the very first night of his reign, when he slipped away from the celebrations to spend a little time with a mistress.

Widespread relief at the relaxation of Puritan restrictions, however, meant members of society, like liberated felons, went about with gay abandon. Gambling, prostitution and promiscuity caused some to question the good of such freedom. Even the liberal-minded civil servant Samuel Pepys looked down his nose at 'the lewdness and beggary of the court which I am feared will bring all to ruin again.'

Not all spokesmen for the Puritan ideal had disappeared underground. When the poet, John Milton, retired from politics at the Restoration of the monarchy to concentrate on poetry, he produced one of the longest laments in the English language on the desperate state of society.

With his eyes deteriorating into blindness, he dictated 10,500 lines in *Paradise Lost* to 'justify the ways of God to men', sadly conceding that Satan is the most beguiling of characters.

Two calamities occurred at about the same time which confirmed to many the truth of the poet's vision. For 18 months from the spring of 1665, England was in the grip of its worst outbreak of the plague since the Black Death three centuries earlier. At its peak, the epidemic was claiming 7,000 Londoners a week, and it spread mercilessly across the country.

Scarcely had the plague died down than a second disaster struck, in the Great Fire of September 1666. Some with fervid imagination noted that without the first numeral of the year, the remaining figure pointed to the apocalyptic anti-Christ of *The Revelation of St John*. Perhaps the wrath of retribution was indeed being visited on this licentious land!

Fleeing into Exile Disguised as a Girl
The brief reign of James II

W hen the Catholic James II came to the throne in 1685, aged 52, he had spent most of his life abroad in exile. As the second son, and one of six children, born to Charles I and the French Henrietta Maria, James spent his adolescence dodging anti-royalists in the Civil War.

He escaped from house arrest in St James's Palace disguised as a girl and fled first to Holland to be with his sister Mary, and then to Paris

to be with his mother (the French king's daughter), and finally to Scotland. Later he joined the French and Spanish armies, before at last retunring to England when his elder brother Charles II had restored the monarchy.

However, James's accession to the throne in 1685 was opposed by many in the Commons who feared the return of Catholicism in government (Roman Catholics had been excluded from the House of Commons since 1678). Coupled with a haughty arrogance, this meant James only lasted three years as king.

The birth of his son, and therefore another Catholic heir, proved an unpalatable prospect for many parliamentarians, who instead invited an invasion from William of Orange, the Protestant son of James's sister Mary, who had married the sovereign prince of Holland.

Declared abdicated, the king, with an all too vivid memory of what had happened to his father, soon fled into exile again – this time to the colourful French milieu of Louis XIV where he would live out much of his remaining life.

JACOBITE REBELLIONS

*When Parliament forced James II to abdicate in favour of William of Orange, supporters of the old Stuart regime were bent on reversing their fortunes. Largely Catholic, though also including some Protestants who did not accept the new Orange regime, these supporters were known as Jacobites (after **Jacobus**, the Latin for James).*

A year after his dethronement, James attempted to recover the crown in 1689, landing in Ireland with a large French army, joined by numerous Jacobite sympathisers. On July 1, a Jacobite army of 21,000 mostly French and Irish troops massed on the south bank of the River Boyne outside Dublin, while William and his army of 35,000 confronted them from the north. The King's superior forces proved too great, however, and James was forced to flee the bogs. The Orange Order still commemorates the victory, erroneously said to have occurred on July 12, hence their reference to 'The Glorious Twelfth'. Any Jacobite hopes of reclaiming the English throne were thus stalled.

James's son, the 'Old Pretender', did join another doomed effort in 1715. The cause was then left to James's grandson, the 'Young Pretender', Bonnie Prince Charlie, to take up the mantle in the 'Forty-Five Rebellion', but this brave effort eventually petered out after defeat at the Battle of Culloden in 1746.

Unlikely Double Act
Mary distraught at having to marry unattractive William

M ary II was the daughter of James duke of York (later James II) by his first wife, Lady Anne Hyde, who died when Mary was still only nine. Although her mother bore eight children, only Mary and her younger sister Anne (future Queen Anne) survived into adulthood. Unlike her father, who converted to Catholicism when she was six, Mary and Anne continued in the Protestant faith, as demanded by her uncle Charles II who was still king.

When, aged 15, Mary was told she would have to marry a foreigner eleven years her elder whom she had never met, she wept for days. Even learning he was her cousin from the House of Orange in Holland made it no better. Indeed she was reported to have cried her eyes out at the wedding. The man in question, William, was hardly an attractive prospect, being asthmatic, stooped, shy and rather quiet – hardly one to lead the Glorious Revolution of 1688-9.

Peaceful revolution
But as Mary would discover when she became queen of England in a joint monarchy with William III, this man had virtues. Indeed, as far as Parliament was concerned he was perfect for the English throne: a reasonable, malleable and, above all, Protestant immigrant, with none of the previous baggage about divine right to rule. Recent events that had led to James II's forced abdication had shaken the government. Now was an opportunity to fix things.

THE MASSACRE OF GLENCOE
After the overthrow of James II there remained in Scotland a stubborn loyalty to the Stuart cause. To pre-

empt any rebellion, William ordered
all Scottish chieftains to swear an
oath of allegiance to the Crown.
He deliberately chose a mid-winter
deadline of December 31, 1691, at the
remote stronghold of Fort William
(named after the English king).
Most obeyed, but the MacDonalds
of Glencoe, delayed by bad weather,
were a few days late. William's
government wished to make an
example of them and ordered their

erstwhile enemy, the Campbells, to
carry out reprisals. After enjoying
a fortnight of traditional Highland
hospitality with the MacDonalds,
one morning before dawn the
Campbell troops massacred the clan
chief and 38 of his men, women and
children in one of the most savage
acts in Scottish history.

Unlike the horrific French
Revolution a century later, the
English people managed simply
to swap one king for another in a
bloodless takeover. Then over the
course of several years they managed
to amend the constitution in their
favour – all under the auspices of a
willing, benign monarchy.

Tragically, Mary died of smallpox
in 1694 and William continued to
reign alone. Much of the king's time
was taken up with European politics
and war, especially endeavouring to
limit France's imperial ambitions in
Western Europe and to safeguard his
native Holland. While these matters
preoccupied the king, Parliament was
free to concentrate on drafting key
changes to the constitution to their
advantage.

Tinkering with the Constitution

On coming to the throne, William and Mary had had to agree to a Declaration of Rights, the terms of which effectively established a limited monarchy. The king or queen was no longer allowed, as James II had been, to exercise a royal prerogative in ignoring any inconvenient laws. The monarch was not above the law.

The Commons also put themselves in charge of royal expenditure. And to prevent any further instability from religious cause, as happened again in the previous regime, the Act of Settlement required all future monarchs to be members of the Church of England.

One further development during the reign of William and Mary was the creation of the Bank of England, in 1694. This became a privately owned establishment, set up as an official fund-raiser for the Government. Its first task was to rebuild the navy which had been decimated by the French in the Battle of Beachy Head – not a popular topic for English history lessons!

Anne Bears More Children Than Any Other English Queen
Yet none to continue Stuart line

It was sadly appropriate that Queen Anne – the last Stuart to rule Britain – was born in 1665, the year of the Great Plague. Her life was to be overshadowed by tragedy and ill-health.

Anne's great sorrow was her inability to bear living children: 17 pregnancies in 16 years left her with no heir and a shattered constitution.

Her only child to survive infancy died aged eleven. By the time she succeeded her brother-in-law, William III, to the throne in 1702 at the age of 37, she was an obese invalid suffering frequent pain from gout and convulsive fits.

Being rendered immobile at times by her condition, the Queen had to be moved about on chairs and by pulleys – even to be lowered through trap doors. As a result, she led a largely sedentary life, disliking the outdoors, and restricting herself to public appearances only when necessary.

It was Queen Anne who is largely responsible for turning Bath into a fashionable resort for the aristocracy. Her visit in 1702 to 'take the waters', which were deemed to have healing qualities, set the trend for Georgian society.

Despite her misfortunes, Anne was a popular and conscientious ruler with a devoted husband in Prince George of Denmark. The alliance she made with her sister Mary against their father, James II, later left Anne with guilty feelings. By way of compensation, perhaps, she reigned with fairness and consideration for

different opinions in politics. She is credited with overseeing the Act of Union of Scotland and England in 1707, which has persisted to the present day, and also the acquisition of territorial gains which laid the foundation of the British Empire.

But Anne's failure to produce an heir spelled the end of the Stuart dynasty when she died in 1714. The throne would pass to a stranger who spoke no English.

German Prince Beats Rivals to the Throne
The English non-plussed with George I

The Elector of Hanover's pronouncement, 'This is a very odd country', on the day after his arrival in England in 1714, was hardly likely to endear him to his new subjects.

England may well have seemed odd to a 55 year-old German prince, whose life revolved around autocratic rule and keen soldiering in a small northern principality. Odder still was the way in which he came to be King of England. He was brought to the throne by an Act of Parliament, which had ignored the better claims of more than 50 other candidates in order to ensure a Protestant succession.

And looking back, one might well wonder at the decision. Georg, or George, as he would now spell his name, spoke virtually no English and made no effort to master the language either, preferring to communicate with his ministers in French or Latin.

He became unpopular with his subjects who thought his appearance and manners very strange. Dressed in a ginger wig and sporting a bright red complexion, his impression was made still more bizarre by his entourage. Two of the ugliest mistresses ever seen in court accompanied him on each arm, one grossly overweight, who was promptly nicknamed 'Elephant', the other anorexically thin, dubbed

'Maypole'. Was there a wife? Yes, but locked up in a German castle having been discovered consorting with a Swedish count. Two swarthy Turks also accompanied the new king as body-servants.

Furthermore, George made little attempt to conceal the love he had for his homeland, which he visited as often as possible. Indeed he spent more time there than in England, and in fact died on one of those visits back to Germany. Such was the people's disaffection for him that there was no incentive even to give the monarch an English burial. The nation simply moved on.

FIRST PRIME MINISTER

The rise to political power of a country squire, Robert Walpole, had much to do with the power vacuum created by an absentee monarch. The new German King of Great Britain needed the good advice and guidance available from the likes of this able and shrewd administrator. Following the financial crash caused by the South Sea Bubble crisis, in which a company failed to honour its promise to pay off the National Debt, Walpole was one of the few parliamentarians to emerge from the scandal unscathed. In taking on two government posts, Chancellor of the Exchequer and First Lord of the Treasury, Walpole elevated himself far higher than any of his peers. This dominance prompted his enemies to give him the title of 'Prime Minister', intended as a term of abuse, but it became an office that was soon to pass into the British way of life. Walpole held the position from 1721 to 1742, and during that time took Britain to new levels of prosperity at home and kept a good peace abroad.

Useful Conformist
George II is meat and drink to Robert Walpole

On acceding to the British throne, George II vowed to transform the monarchy from the dull, remote and Germanic flavour his father had created. As a mark of his intentions, the new king demanded a magnificent coronation with Handel playing his great anthem, *Zadok the Priest and Nathan the Prophet Crowned*

Solomon King. The music has been played at every British coronation since.

George II's determination to be a better monarch than his father comes largely from his background. This last English monarch to be born abroad had a miserable childhood. Aged eleven, he saw his mother incarcerated for an alleged affair. He is unlikely to have ever seen her again, though he did once try to swim the moat of the castle where she was being kept prisoner, but

George II in coronation robes

was unsuccessful. Once brought to England, George maintained a hatred of his father who would never allow him to do anything for himself.

When George married the German princess Caroline, they kept well away from the old king, biding their time until his death, upon which, it is said, the young George rejoiced wholeheartedly.

Though different from his father in many ways, George II still had instilled in him the Germanic passion for method. Business or pleasure, all had to conform to a strict routine – he was often to be found outside his mistress's room, watch in hand, waiting for the hour of nine to chime.

Duping the king

His wife Caroline was a forceful character with a lively intelligence. Once Prime Minister Walpole realised she wore the trousers in their relationship, he weaselled his way into her confidence. Caroline's ambition and vanity made her a sucker for Walpole's flattery.

Together they manipulated the king to follow Walpole's policies. The two would meet in secret, Walpole divulging his political ideas. The Queen would talk in private with her husband before he interviewed the Prime Minster, believing he had new ideas to present. Walpole duly humoured the King and went away with approval for what were in fact his own policy initiatives. In this way, Walpole and Caroline ruled the country. Indeed it was effectively Walpole doing the running.

Meanwhile George increasingly took a back seat in government, going off on longer breaks to Hanover in a manner reminiscent of his father. His 'reign', if that is what it can be called, lasted for 33 years. During it, his government ministers increased considerably Britain's strength and influence abroad. George II was the last king to be buried in Westminster Abbey and was succeeded by his grandson because his own son, Frederick, had died in an accident while playing cricket.

THE FLOWERING OF GEORGIAN SOCIETY

Political stability in the Hanoverian period allowed 18th century life to bloom into a colourful exuberance.

The upper classes became eccentric, sophisticated and, above all, they loved gossip. One dandy, Beau Nash, became the renowned 'Arbiter of Elegance'. From his unofficial 'thronedom' in the spa town of Bath, Nash laid down rules of etiquette which the rest of society – meaning the aristocracy – followed. One book gave instructions on 'How to take off your Hat and replace it'. Correct manners complimented correct appearance: in George II's reign, officers in the British army used 65,000 tons of flour every year for powdering wigs.

Struggle for Power
George III faces the realities of a modernising democracy

Stubborn, simple and well meaning, George III ascended the throne in 1760 determined to follow his mother's advice to 'be a king'. Being unusually British-born for a Hanoverian, he believed he possessed something his two predecessors lacked – the ability to understand the turbulent nation he had been called upon to lead.

George III was convinced that his two predecessors had been tricked by unscrupulous politicians – the Whigs – into giving up many of the customary rights of a king. He was determined to assert himself and claw back power to the crown.

But such determination could not conceal a degree of naivety about the task ahead. The world was marching to a new order with the rising Industrial Revolution. Prosperity was spreading into the Midlands and the North as the innovations of water-power and then steam power brought new found wealth – and with it political power. As the mill-owner Joseph Arkwright boasted, his

invention, the spinning frame, could 'pay off the National Debt' on its own. There was no doubt power was shifting into the hands of industrial businessmen, and the king had to realise that.

At the same time, the British Empire was fast expanding. Victory in the Seven Years' War (1756-63) won vast new territories in Canada and India, while Captain Cook discovered Australia. Amid the general euphoria roused by these conquests, there was one demoralising failure: the loss of America. George's ebullient rule was not used to failure.

Failure in America

When the American colonies rebelled against British rule, the king declared he would rather lose his crown than abandon the empire. With a one-track mind George pursued a hardline policy, refusing to make concessions.

This attitude was typified by the government's famous effort to ruin American tea merchants in 1773. Having dispatched a ship of the East India Company laden with tea to Boston, the government was dismayed to find out that on achoring in

the harbour, the ship's entire cargo was tipped into the sea, an incident dubbed as The Boston Tea Party.

The eventual failure in America, at huge financial cost, severely dented George's self-confidence. His government, led by Prime Minister Lord North, fell and a year of crisis followed. This was ended only by the appointment of a new prime minister in William Pitt who, it was understood, would have to introduce far-reaching reforms. Ultimately these measures spelled the end of royal power as George knew it.

King and Pitt conducted an uneasy alliance out of necessity to prevent the forces of insurrection that seemed to be sparking everywhere around them, notably in France. Fear that revolution could spread across the Channel kept the British government in constant jitters.

Declining health

By the time Britain had ridden out that particular storm, and was triumphing in naval wars against the French and Spanish, George had unfortunately descended into madness. For 50 years he had tried to

In his youth the Prince Regent was renowned for his dashing good looks

dominate events, often striving against the prevailing current. But the last ten years of his reign he spent in isolation at Windsor Castle suffering from a rare disease of the metabolism known as porphyria, or 'flying gout'.

Bouts of violent derangement meant he had to be constrained in a straitjacket within a padded chamber. He would talk incessantly and suffer delusions, claiming to converse with angels. Once when taking fresh air, he addressed a tree as the king of Prussia.

A palliative for the disease was thought to be sea-bathing; and inadvertently his trips to the south coast started a fashion for seaside holidays. Towards the end, exhausted by illness and the travails of a long reign, George III dressed in ragged clothes with trailing white beard, looking more like a crazed king Lear than the genial monarch who had come to the throne.

The Prince Who Lost His Charm
The ungovernable Prince of 'Whales' and George IV

One of the most extraordinary periods in the history of English royalty was the era known as the Regency. It occurred when King George III was absent from rule because of prolonged illness between 1811 and 1820. Power was handed to his son as Prince Regent.

Famous for his extravagant lifestyle, the Prince of Wales started out as a popular man. Tall, handsome, witty and intelligent, he became known as 'the first gentleman of Europe'.

His flamboyance and scandalous life outside court, however, drew more disdain than pride from his disciplined father. The Prince reacted by openly rebelling against the King, delighting in the embarrassment this might cause him. Once, in 1783, the Prince appeared at the state opening of Parliament dressed in:

Black velvet, most richly embroidered with gold, and pink spangles, and lined with pink satin. His shoes had pink heels; his hair was pressed much at the sides, and very full frizzed, with two very small curls at the bottom. (William Gardiner, Music and Friends)

The good times, however, could not last without repercussions. The excesses of a lifesytle of gay abandon took their toll and his body grew inexorably to gigantic proportions. Unfortunately for the Prince of Wales, he lived in an age of political and artistic freedom, and became the natural target of cartoonists who could not resist such a brilliant opportunity to exercise their acerbic talents. Cruickshank referred to him as the 'Prince of Whales'; Gillray entitled a disgusting cartoon, 'A Voluptuary under the Horrors of

Digestion'. The cruel mockery culminated in one of his critics, Leigh Hunt, being imprisoned for two years for seditious libel.

Out of control
In a running battle with his father, the Prince did everything in his power to upset him, including his choice of marriage partner. George III had not long reaffirmed state policy in the Royal Marriages Act stipulating all royal wives be Protestant, when his son presented his wife, whom he had married in secret. She was Mrs Maria Fitzherbert, a commoner, twice widowed – and Roman Catholic.

Furthermore, the Prince refused to spend within the budget agreed by the government. His racing activities alone cost £30,000 a year. The enormity of his debts, which escalated to £640,000, caused great embarrassment at a time when the nation's coffers were already depleted by the Napoleonic Wars.

Deal struck
A strategy was hatched by Prime Minister William Pitt. In return for scrapping his debt, the Prince should

wed again (the first marriage being deemed illegal). This time it would be to an attractive, fashionable young woman of impeccable pedigree, his German cousin Princess Caroline.

But the Prince was not happy. Commissioners were appointed to watch over his expenditure in every detail. As the commentator William Cobbett remarked, 'The prince was placed under a guardianship and control as severe as if he had still been an infant, or something even lower in the scale of intellectual capacity.'

On top of this, he did not like his new wife, who turned out to be as spendthrift as her husband. The ploy backfired. The couple separated, but the Prince's parties continued as riotously as ever, probably as much to irritate his poor father as for any desire for pleasure.

Regency turn

Curiously, once his father was forced to relinquish power of rule and the Regency set up in 1811, the Prince's outlook began to change. As nominal head of state, he now felt too grown up – at nearly 50 – to continue in the role of *enfant terrible*. Instead, the Prince Regent directed his energies into art and architecture.

From his partnership with a dashing designer in John Nash came forth a new style of architecture now known as Regency. He channelled his flair for flamboyance and frippery into buildings, notably the onion-domed Royal Pavilion in Brighton. With Nash they redesigned great swathes of the West End of London, creating Regent Street and Regent's Park, with its 'wedding-cake' terraces. They also remodelled Buckingham Palace.

However, by the time the Prince Regent was crowned king, as George IV in 1820, he was a spent force. The heady lifestyle of his past was over and he withdrew into isolation at Windsor.

Sick and troubled by insomnia, the new King doused himself with large doses of cherry brandy and laudanum to soothe his gout. When George died in 1830 Britain was to lose one of the most controversial kings in its history. As *The Times* newspaper recorded, 'There was never an individual less regretted by his fellow creatures than this deceased king.'

Surprised to be King
Sober William IV is welcome relief

The third son of George III was not expected to become king and so was not trained for monarchy. At the age of 13 he was sent to sea and there he acquired a nautical directness and taste for strong language. He was known for being tactless and earned the original nickname 'Silly Billy'.

William had spent most of his life as a private man, with none of the indulgence his elder brother George

IV enjoyed. He lived quietly with his mistress and actress who mothered their ten illegitimate children. When his other elder brother, Frederick (the 'Grand Old Duke of York') died, and George IV's only child Charlotte had died in childbirth, William suddenly found himself next in line to the throne.

Furthermore, the present king, George IV, was seriously ailing. William had three years to prepare to receive the crown but was certainly chuffed at the idea. He is said to have spent months practising his royal signature, 'William R'.

Although 64 when he did accede, William was in good shape. Being essentially good-natured and compliant, his reign was mostly uneventful. In agreeing to all the government proposals put to him over the Reform Bill of 1832, the King was said by Prime Minister Earl Grey to have behaved 'like an angel'.

William's common-sense attitude to most things helped raise the public estimation of the monarchy. If nothing else, he had rescued it from the depths of scandal to which his brother had plunged it.

Propping Up
The Queen
Victoria and her men

Q ueen Victoria's vital statistics are: married 21 years, widowed 40 years, reigned 64 years; lived 82 years. Once the longest reigning monarch England had ever had, she may also have been the most emotionally troubled. An unhappy childhood, stifling mother and inconsolable bereavement at the loss of Prince Albert undermined the confidence of this most austere Empress of India.

Intimate pictures of Victoria and Albert bely the power struggle between them

Despite her strong sense of sovereignty, in which she alone was ruler of this nation and empire, Victoria always needed a man at her side for support. And it had to be a beautiful one at that. Lord Melbourne was her prime minister in the early days of her reign. In this witty and charming politician she found the kindly advice and almost flirtatious attention that pleased her.

Victoria was constantly in need of reassurance. A deep insecurity stemmed from her earliest days. Her father, Duke of Kent, died when she was just eight months old, and her mother, Princess of Saxe-Coburg-Gotha, believed that Victoria should be shut away from the world and kept under the strictest supervision. She was not even allowed downstairs at home in Kensington Palace without the governess holding her hand.

Becoming queen
The strict code of morality and manners that were to be the hallmark of Victoria's later character were inculcated in this stifling domestic atmosphere. When at table as a young girl, she had to sit with a holly leaf

between ruff and chin to keep her face respectfully upright.

Victoria's loathing for her mother did not vent itself until the day she became queen. Alone after the coronation ceremony, she turned to her and asked, 'And now, Mamma, am I really and truly queen?' Her mother affirmed that she was. 'Then, dear Mamma,' Victoria continued, 'I hope you will grant me the first request I make to you as queen. Let me be by myself for an hour.' This snub was probably as much as her daughter could muster at the time, but it reveals a deep resentment.

Offering comfort and flattery, Lord Melbourne was able to help Victoria overcome her self-doubts and nervousness, easing the transition from Princess to Queen. But despite the elevation in her status, Victoria continued to suffer from the suffocating relationship with her mother, a 'dreadful state' she confessed, and one that could only be remedied by marriage.

Albert of Germany
An initial determination not to marry altered on meeting her cousin, Albert

of Saxe-Coburg-Gotha. Soon after their second encounter, three years later, Victoria was apparently smitten by Albert's lean masculine beauty. She wasted no time and proposed to him, as was her prerogative.

Though uncomfortable in English surroundings, Albert vowed 'to train myself to be a good and useful man'. Scholarly and diligent, he was more at home with books than people; his shyness and inability to master the English language did nothing to help his confidence either.

And what exactly of their love? Their wedding night ended with an early morning walk, hardly the endorsement of a flourishing passion.

The Queen is said to have adored Albert, yet he showed none of the signs of requiting that love.

In reality he suffered miserably from her dominance – she had insisted on keeping the word 'obey' in his marriage vow – and was refused any real power in state affairs. The business of ruling was hers alone. She allowed him to blot her papers for her, as a concession, but did not make him consort until 1857 when the last of their nine children was born – and only then when she realised that her son Edward, in whom both parents were disappointed, would otherwise succeed to the throne.

The frustration Albert felt is apparent from his diary. Once he wrote of his difficulties: 'She will not hear me out but flies into a rage and overwhelms me with reproaches of suspiciousness, want of trust, envy, etc.' This does not sound like a loving relationship.

Role reversal

With her increasing confinement for child-bearing, Victoria came to cede more and more power to Albert, causing a curious reversal of roles. She became submissive and withdrawn, he overbearing, coldly rational and unforgiving of her frequent outbursts. Victoria suffered from depression, Albert from emotional isolation.

Having finally yielded so much to her supportive husband, on whom she came to depend utterly, Victoria was devastated by his death from typhoid fever in 1861.

The Queen wore widow's weeds for the remaining 40 years of her life. She refused to have her room changed in the slightest detail, except for the fresh flowers she strewed over his bed every day. Even five years after his death, Victoria excused herself from opening Parliament because she did not wish to be the 'spectacle of a poor, broken-hearted widow, nervous and shrinking, dragged in deep mourning.'

John Brown

Alas one more man would come into her life, in the unexpected form of John Brown, a no-nonsense Scottish Highlander who referred to her as 'wumman'. He too became her prop, which she needed now more than ever before. Nobody was allowed to speak to her, except through Brown as her intermediary. Such was her dependence that she even tolerated his heavy bouts of whisky drinking.

Pleasure Seeker
Edward VII epitomises age of excitement

With the death of Queen Victoria in 1901, Britain entered a new era. For many it was an age of unbridled pleasure. The restraints the old queen had symbolised were now thrown off in an access of exuberant recreation.

No one epitomised this new mood better than the new king, Edward VII, despite his 60 years of age. His

obvious enjoyment of the good things in life – enormous cigars, racehorses and attractive women – set the tone of social life across the classes.

The first motorcars were being driven, music halls were packed with loud audiences around Piccadilly Circus. The invention of the radio and wind-up gramophones brought stirring patriotic songs by Elgar into Edwardian parlours. And throughout the country the earliest images on celluloid flickered across new cinema screens. The King himself was the first monarch to win the Derby.

Despite a sense of fun that Edward brought to the court, he was also capable of diplomacy and a certain amount of work – despite the academic laziness he exhibited as a youth.

Indeed he had long shed his early playboy image to pursue peace. His visits to France were well received and paved the way for the Entente Cordiale of 1904. Astute and perceptive, Edward was one of the few monarchs in Europe who could foresee the coming storm clouds that would burst into world war.

Hanover Dropped
*George V endeavours to keep
onside in wartime strife*

George V was unfortunate in having to lead his country through the First World War. He was doubly unfortunate to have German ancestry and relatives in the enemy camp.

When anti-German feelings were running at their highest in 1917, George decided enough was enough. Great fondness he might have had for his cousin Wilhelm II, but duty to the nation came first. In a momentous act

that brought greater change to the monarchy than at any time since the Glorious Revolution, the King made two radical revisions.

Firstly he renamed the dynasty 'Windsor', thus symbolically removing their attachment to the German Hanover. By the same token any aristocrats with Germanic names were required to change theirs, for example Battenberg to Mountbatten.

The second alteration to the monarchy was still more radical. Not only did George change the name, he dropped the Hanoverian custom that marriage partners should have

George V enjoyed taking the helm aboard his favourite royal yacht, Britannia

aristocratic status. From now on British monarchs were free to marry whoever they liked, as long as they were not Catholic or divorced.

In one stroke George had both anglicised and broadened the monarchy. A royal wedding would now become a marriage of love, not a political affair, and the royal family would be taken as a model of family life. This, as future generations would discover, was a mistaken ideal.

The king himself was therefore the last English monarch to have an arranged marriage. His mother, Queen Victoria, decided he should marry Princess May of Teck (later known as Queen Mary), who had been engaged to George's elder brother Eddy before he died prematurely. Fortunately it turned out to be a good match.

Social progress

George himself found developments happening in British society hard to accept, and more than a little worrying. The royal family had suffered great shock at the violent overthrow of the Russian monarchy in 1917, in which George's cousin,

Tsar Nicholas II and his family, had perished. Now civil unrest was afflicting his country. The working class movement and the General Strike of 1926, the demand for equality from the Suffragettes, some even going on hunger strike, another dying when she hurled herself at the king's horse in the Epsom Derby, and not to mention the first Labour Government – these were all elements of a new political order at odds with the King's own traditional culture.

George V was an old-fashioned stickler for routine and ritual. He always went to bed at 11.10 pm, demanded his sons wore morning dress when visiting him, and expected the servants to ensure no furniture was ever an inch out of its correct position. At his favourite residence of Sandringham in Norfolk, the clocks were all set half an hour fast to ensure he could never be late.

It was from here that George broadcast his historic first Christmas message in 1932. It was a great publicity coup. For the first time in British history the monarch could wish his subjects a Merry Christmas.

Eligible Bachelor Becomes Figure of Mistrust
Edward VIII's fall from grace

Dashing and debonair, Edward Prince of Wales, eldest son of George V and heir apparent, was regarded by society as the most eligible bachelor in the world. The Prince toured the British Empire at the end of the First World War and joined Europe's high society. He even set new trends in fashion with his trouser zip-fly, the Windsor knot in his tie, plus-fours on the golf course, and wearing no shirt on the beach.

It was a time of new found freedom, having spent his childhood restrained by the strict conventions and hallowed traditions observed by his parents. Parties, nightclubs, casinos and weekends in the country were meat and drink to Edward, and he had a string of affairs, often with married women. In short, Edward relished the carefree life which had been denied him as a child.

But with it also came a dislike of duty which he found 'bothersome'. It became clear that while this man lapped up the adulation of crowds, he felt uncomfortable in any formal situation, disliking, for example, speaking in public.

Mrs Simpson

When Edward first met the American Mrs Simpson in 1931 she seemed to make little impact on him. But a year later, after being invited to dinner with the Simpsons (she and her second husband), he fell hopelessly in love with Wallis. Quite rapidly he fell under her spell in an infatuation that seemed to deprive him of most independent decision-making. The Prince's equerry wrote in 1934, 'Edward has lost all

confidence in himself and follows W around like a dog'.

When his father died in January 1936, Edward succeeded as king in what must have been a reluctant state of mind. He was hardly ever seen without Mrs Simpson on his arm. The affair with this woman, who had subsequently divorced her second husband, was common knowledge but generated a nervous silence in public. The press voluntarily kept out of their affairs.

Though Edward was at liberty to marry a commoner if he so wished, the Church of England refused to bless the marriage of divorcees. Therefore Mrs Simpson could not become queen, yet Edward as king was 'Supreme Governor of the Church of England'. The dilemma was his.

Finally pressure mounted in December that year when Bishop Blunt of Bradford made public comment on the king's 'need for grace'. This came at the end of a year when much had happened to affect world politics: Hitler had marched into the Rhineland, Mussolini's troops had conquered Ethiopia, and the

Spanish Civil War had broken out. Britain now needed strong leadership, not dithering. It was Stanley Baldwin, the Prime Minister, who forced Edward's hand. In an unprecedented move, Edward VIII put his own private life before his duty to the nation, and abdicated.

It must have been a huge relief for him, and Mrs Simpson. Immediately Edward went into 'exile' abroad, never to return. The couple married the following year.

Nazi sympathiser

Quite how much Edward was influenced by Mrs Simpson, who undoubtedly was a forceful character, has led to some claiming she was a German spy charged with the task of endearing the former king to side with Hitler. In 1937, the couple famously visited the Fuhrer and found much to admire in his social reforms. Edward is said to have even given the Nazi salute to Hitler. Clearly there was a propaganda opportunity for the Nazis if Edward could fall into partnership with Germany as a puppet-king in the waiting. His brother Albert, now the new king as

George VI, ensured no such banner should be flown in England, and the ex-king found himself permanently banished to the political wilderness.

Fearless in War, Fearful in Life
Stuttering Bertie becomes the people's champion

The life of George VI is a story of two halves. His early life was one of subjugation. Having an elder brother as glamorous as Edward VIII who set the world alight was always going to put Albert Frederick Arthur George in the shadows. But a lack of intelligence and chronic sickness compounded a sense of inferiority, which was not helped by being given the nickname, Bertie (he was only named Albert because his birthday fell on the anniversary of the death of Queen Victoria's consort).

George developed a stammer and became heavily addicted to cigarettes and alcohol, which only undermined his health. But the Prince of York made it into the navy despite coming bottom in the college entrance exams. A determination to

come up to the mark in the First World War was constantly checked by seasickness and bouts of gastritis (a legacy from his childhood due to poor diet and negligence at the hands of his nurse). In the crucial Battle of Jutland in 1916 – the year when he had a duodenal ulcer diagnosed – the Prince managed to salvage some pride by leaving his sickbed to fight in the gun turret of HMS Collingwood.

This single act of heroism marked a threshold in the Prince's life: he had proved to himself he was more capable than he imagined. In a letter

George VI never felt so at ease as when he was on duty in the navy

to his brother, Bertie revealed, 'When I was on top of the turret, I never felt any fear of shells or anything else.'

Becoming king

But this achievement was as nothing compared to what was asked of him in 1936 when Edward VIII abdicated, leaving the crown to Bertie. The nation drew its breath and prayed. 'I never wanted this to happen. I'm only a naval officer, it's the only thing I know about,' he confided to his cousin Lord Louis Mountbatten on the first night of his reign.

Never expected to be king, the Prince of York was completely unprepared for the job, having never handled a state document in his life. Yet, the courage he summoned at Jutland he could summon again. The first thing he did was dispense with that humiliating nickname. Instead he chose his last Christian name, George, in a gesture of continuity with his father after the disastrous failure of his brother. With medical assistance the new king mastered his embarrassing stammer and within a few years of his accession had endeared the public to him.

Perhaps the greatest boon to his self-esteem came from the devotion and support of his wife Lady

Elizabeth Bowes-Lyon, to whom he was married in a genuine union of love. Together they faced the challenges posed by another world war. To show moral support for their embattled subjects, the royal family remained in London during the thunderous air raids of the Blitz. Two bombs landed on Buckingham Palace, exploding just 30 metres from the King – the queen consort famously remarked to a policeman the next day, 'I'm glad we've been bombed. It makes me feel I can look the East End in the face'.

The King and queen restricted themselves to the same regime of rationing as their fellow citizens had to follow. Day after day during the early years of the war, when England had her back to the wall, the couple tried to keep up morale by visiting bombed out areas of the East End and evacuees sheltering in the London Underground.

Come VE Day, the outcome was a triumph for both nation and king. Alongside his people, George VI had stood the test of character, and in recognition of the many instances of civilian heroism he introduced the

George Cross and Medal. The King had undoubtedly had a good war. He was fortunate too in having a good leader in Winston Churchill who could do most of the talking. But in George VI, Britain can justly claim to have had a king who got the measure of being a monarch in a modern state. Alas, poor health dogged him to the end. George died of arterial disease and lung cancer in 1952, aged 56.

Fashion Icon to Fading Star
Elizabeth II was precocious but could she mother?

Elizabeth's first address to the nation came at the tender age of 14 when her parents, King George VI and Queen Elizabeth, asked her to broadcast to the children during the Blitz of 1940.

This propulsion of Elizabeth into the public eye at such a young age had the effect of generating a large, almost cult following. At every opportunity the Press would eagerly snap pictures of this pretty, vivacious princess who was eminently photogenic. She fast became a fashion

icon. Parents copied her styles in their own daughters, and well into the 1960s girls were habitually dressed in full-skirted frocks with puffed sleeves, lace collar and a sash round the waist. In her many activities too the Princess was emulated, in sports, horse riding, and the Girl Guides. Elizabeth became the emblem of a happy, outdoor royal family life – a welcome distraction from the social and economic problems of the 1930s.

But this all changed quite quickly once her 'Uncle David' (Edward VIII) abdicated and her father became king in 1936. Gone was the carefree joie

de vivre. Relations at home became much more formal. Elizabeth was expected to curtsy to her father every time he came into the room. Rather suddenly, at the age of ten, she was next in line to the throne, and so had to take on state responsibility. While her general education continued apace, much more of her time was now devoted to training to be queen of Britain and the empire.

Though duty came to dominate the Princess's life, she was by all accounts a natural. From an early age Elizabeth had an imperious nature. Once, aged three, when tired of her mother's visitor, she rang for the footman and said, 'Kindly ring for a taxi. Our guest is leaving.' She knew her own mind even in love. From the moment she set eyes on Prince Philip of Greece at the age of 13, she fell madly in love; only her father's iron will persuaded her to delay the wedding until she was 21.

Rival commitments

In becoming the nation's sovereign in 1952 Elizabeth naturally threw all her energies into monarchical duties. Far behind her were the days of being a fashion queen. She had a four-year-old son, Charles, and a two-year-old daughter, Anne. After taking a period off childbearing, she resumed with the births of Andrew and Edward in the 1960s. It has been suggested that Elizabeth may have found running the monarchy more to her liking than running a family, that she was intolerant of those who did not match up to her own high standards, and that perhaps her children did not receive as much emotional support as they needed while growing through the tender years of childhood.

Certainly, three divorces out of four marriages, including that of the heir to the throne, has not brought a happy complexion to the House of Windsor. The similarity between her own exuberant youth and that of the person who derailed the monarchy is striking. Like Elizabeth, Diana, Princess of Wales, became the glamorous photogenic captive of the paparazzi; the essential difference that Elizabeth put duty first, Diana her personal happiness.

As the monarchy's sacrificial victim, Diana was able to exploit public sympathies in her favour. In contrast, the Queen appeared cold, frumpy and distinctly out of touch with her people – perhaps for the first time in her life. It took some time after the death of Diana before the Queen was back on good terms with her subjects. This marked a rare misjudgement in the career of an inspirational head of state whose own record is otherwise without blemish. As bearer of the royal standard, guardian of all the cherished traditions that represent the British monarchy today, Elizabeth II is said never to have made a faux pas in all the long years of her reign.

INDEX

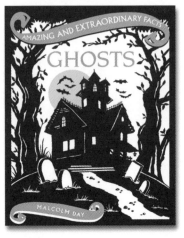

Amazing and Extraordinary
Facts Series: Ghosts
Malcom Day
ISBN: 978-1 -910821-183

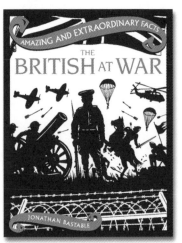

Amazing and Extraordinary
Facts Series: The British
At War
Jonathan Bastable
ISBN: 978-1 -910821-237

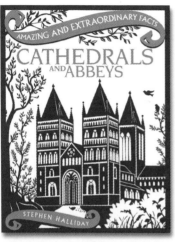

Amazing and Extraordinary
Facts Series: Cathedrals &
Abbeys
Stephen Halliday
ISBN: 978-1 -910821-046

Amazing and Extraordinary
Facts Series: Churchill
Joseph Piercy
ISBN: 978-1 -910821-077

For more great books visit our website at **www.rydonpublishing.co.uk**